MW00513643

With Our Eyes on Jesus

Devotions on the Minor Festivals of the Church Year

Richard E. Lauersdorf

Cover photos by Adobe Image Library and Planet Art.

"I Hear the Savior Calling," stanza 5, by John C. Lawrenz, is used with permission on page 72.

All Scripture quotations, unless otherwise indicated, are taken from the HOLY BIBLE, NEW INTERNATIONAL VERSION®. NIV®. Copyright © 1973, 1978, 1984 by International Bible Society. Used by permission of Zondervan Publishing House. All rights reserved.

The "NIV" and "New International Version" trademarks are registered in the United States Patent and Trademark Office by International Bible Society. Use of either trademark requires the permission of International Bible Society.

All rights reserved. No part of this publication may be reproduced, stored in a retrieval system, or transmitted in any form or by any means—electronic, mechanical, photocopying, recording, or otherwise—except for brief quotations in reviews, without prior permission from the publisher.

Library of Congress Control Number 00-133302
Northwestern Publishing House
1250 N. 113th St., Milwaukee, WI 53226-3284
© 2000 by Northwestern Publishing House
Published 2000
Printed in the United States of America
ISBN 0-8100-1243-X

Contents

Foreword

Turn to the last pages of this little volume, and you'll find them listed. They are called the minor festivals of the church year, but we seldom hear sermons or read devotions based on them. In our desire to focus on Christ and his saving work, we have stepped away from observing the days of the saints and other festivals. Yet next to Easter and Pentecost, some of these minor festivals were the oldest fixed dates in the calendar and liturgy of the church.

The early church understood the close connection between the cross of Christ and the lives of the saints in Christ. So did the reformer Martin Luther. He wrote, "For [in the lives of the saints] one is greatly pleased to find how they sincerely believed God's Word, confessed it with their lips, praised it by their living, and honored and confirmed it by their suffering and dying" (*What Luther Says,* Vol. 3, p. 1251).

Here were believers who by God's grace had eyes fixed on Jesus (Hebrews 12:2). By God's grace they knew and followed Jesus, listening to, loving, and living out his Word. By God's grace they did and dared for Jesus, even, for many of them, to the point of laying down their lives for their Savior. Reflecting on what Scripture says about the saints is seeing revealed in bold detail the greatness of God's amazing grace in Christ Jesus.

May the God of all grace fix our eyes on Jesus through the devotions on the minor festivals of the church, which this book humbly presents.

The Name of Jesus

On the eighth day, when it was time to circumcise him, he was named Jesus, the name the angel had given him before he had been conceived. (Luke 2:21)

Entering the New Year in Jesus' Name

The doorbell kept ringing at 2:00 A.M. that New Year's morning. On the porch stood a college student from the congregation. His father had died tragically when the student was just a little boy, and life had never been the same. There the young man stood, eyes full of despair, breath reeking of alcohol, about to end his own life rather than face another year filled with the same doubts and despair.

What to tell him? Thank God his Spirit guides, as he has promised. Along with coffee that early morning, the troubled Christian received the assurance of what the new year could be when entered in Jesus' name. We need the same assurance. When we enter the new year in Jesus' name, it will be . . .

A year filled with his forgiveness

Nothing unusual happened that day in Bethlehem. An eight-day-old boy was circumcised as countless others had been in the 19-some centuries since God had come to Abraham and commanded it. Even the name Jesus, given this little boy at his circumcision, was not uncommon. Others had carried it, including the famous Joshua who had led the Israelites across the River Jordan. Nothing unusual in all this, that is, to the outward eye.

But to the eye of the believer, what a scene! That baby going under the knife in circumcision is God himself, who took on our human flesh, took up the load of our sins, took them to Calvary's cross, and there took them away forever, so that he could take us to heaven. As part of that act of redemption, the circumcision knife spills drops of his precious blood, promise of the crimson tide that would later stain the sand on Calvary's hill. Also as part of that act of redemption, the holy Jesus, who had no original sin and therefore no need for the covenant of God's grace into which circumcision ushered, undergoes it that he might fulfill God's laws in our place. Many before him bore the name Jesus with its meaning "The Lord Saves," but it truly fits this eight-day-old.

What will the new year bring for us? More sin? Of course, in spite of our efforts to resist as believers. Looking in the rearview mirror, we see how much sin has littered the highway of the year gone by. Like soiled paper and shattered glass, our thoughts, words, and deeds dot the ditches. Thank God we have a Savior who does more than gather up those sins into orange plastic bags for someone to haul off to some landfill somewhere. His forgiveness is so complete and the delete key on his computer so effective that those sins are gone in his eyes as if they never happened.

The same will hold true in all the days of any other year God allows us to experience. Let the devil attack us with the threat of our sins, as he did that young student on my front porch that New Year's Day. "The blood of Jesus, his Son, purifies us from all sin" (1 John 1:7). At his circumcision God's Son received the name Jesus; at our baptisms we received a new name as his saved people. Because his name fit, so does ours. Because God has promised forgiveness, it will be there for us as penitent sinners.

A year filled with his faithfulness

In Genesis chapter 17 when God gave Abraham the rite of circumcision, he intended it also as a sign that his promise to send the Savior would come true. Just think of it. Over the centuries the Jewish male, from eight days on, carried on his body a sign of God's faithfulness. Over those centuries many in Israel forgot what the sign meant. They centered on the act itself instead of on the promised Savior, to whose coming it pointed. After the Savior's coming, some in Israel still misunderstood, demanding the continuation of circumcision instead of rejoicing in the Savior who had come. But through all those years, God had not forgotten. When the fullness of his time had come, he sent forth his Son. God's faithfulness is beyond question, as that eight-day-old Jesus on the day of his circumcision reminds us.

What will the new year hold for us? More trouble and trial? Of course—for some of us more than we might imagine. This past year some of us, like that young man on my front porch, raised tear-stained eyes toward heaven, wondering if our God was too busy numbering the stars and managing the universe to pay attention to our needs and fears. Yet he is always there, just as he promised. His commanding voice stilled the storms or enabled us to stay the course. His gentle touch brushed away the tears and brought comfort in our grief. His wise counsel gave us answers and guided our actions. And here we are with one year ended and another beginning.

Want to enter the new year in Jesus' name? There's only one way. Go to the Word! There our God of all grace continues to assure us of his forgiveness and faithfulness.

Prayer: Thank you, Lord, for sending your Son to be our Savior. May his name Jesus assure us that you have washed us clean from all sin through his blood and thus help us enter a new year with confidence. Sure of your forgiveness, help us also be sure of your faithfulness in guiding and guarding us each new day. In Jesus' name we ask it. Amen.

"But what about you?" he asked. "Who do you say I am?"

Simon Peter answered, "You are the Christ, the Son of the living God."

Jesus replied, "Blessed are you, Simon son of Jonah, for this was not revealed to you by man, but by my Father in heaven. And I tell you that you are Peter, and on this rock I will build my church, and the gates of Hades will not overcome it." (Matthew 16:15-18)

Standing on Firm Ground

People who go ice fishing in our part of the country can hardly wait to get out on the lake. Every winter one or two become impatient. And they end up going out onto the lake but, sometimes, into it—often with fatal results. There's just no substitute for firm ice.

How much more true when it comes to our salvation. When the serious matter of reaching heaven safely is involved, we want to be standing on firm ground.

No other foundation

"Who do people say the Son of Man is?" Jesus had asked his disciples. Echoing the "Gallup polls" of the day, they answered, "John the Baptist," "Elijah," "Jeremiah." Opinions were a dime a dozen. And just six months before the cross. How tragic!

Then came the key question: "But what about you? Who do you say I am?" Ever ready to step forward, Peter spoke up, "You are the Christ, the Son of the living God." Oh, Peter, for a change you've got it right. That's no John the Baptist or Elijah or Jeremiah you've been following for almost three years. That's no mere mortal or prestigious prophet you've seen replace water with wine for an embarrassed bridal couple, restore a daughter to a grief-stricken father, receive with forgiveness a shamed and scorned woman. That's "the Christ, the Son of the living God." He's the one promised since sin closed Eden's door, the Christ who would open heaven's door with his perfect sacrifice on the cross. He's the Son of the living God, come into human flesh to do what only God could do. With his blood he would vaporize the wall of sin, which stretched from hell to heaven and which no sinner could crawl under, crash through, or climb over. Yes, bless you, Peter, for your marvelous confession.

Do we hear how Jesus described Peter's confession? "Rock," he called it. Though the Roman Catholic Church claims that Peter is the rock on which Jesus built his church, the Greek language, which Jesus spoke, makes that interpretation impossible. In Greek *Peter* means "rock" and is masculine in form, while "this rock" is feminine, obviously not referring to Simon Peter. Not Peter but his confession was the rock. Not the one who spoke but the truth he spoke was the firm foundation for Christ's church.

What must Christ say when he looks at what some have tried to do to this firm foundation? The air hammers of human reason have been chattering away at Scripture's central truth of salvation alone by God's grace through Christ's redemptive work. The relentless acid of postmodern society, with its emphasis on what you feel is what you believe, not what some book tries to tell you, keeps eating away at the rock on which Christ said he builds his church. No matter! "This rock" still stands and will continue to stand, regardless of what Satan and hell try against it.

Equally important, our eternal future still stands. Those who stand on Christ the rock will see heaven.

No other faith

Yes, Peter, what a confession! But that confession was not your own doing. Your feet stand on Christ only because the Father in heaven reveals the truth and gives faith to believe it. "Blessed" is the right word, and Peter or "rock" is the right name for you now, all because of what your gracious God has done for you.

What does the only Savior see when he looks at you and me? Hopefully, not just an "inherited faith," which blithely assumes faith can be transferred automatically from parents to children. Hopefully, not just a "confirmation faith," which is satisfied with knowing some facts and reciting some passages. Hopefully, not just an "institutional faith," which takes refuge in belonging to some church body. But someone equally blessed by the Father as Peter was, someone who can answer with the heart of faith, "You are the Christ, the Son of the living God, *my Savior.*"

When's the last time we thanked the Father for this gift of faith? Remember, only those who believe in Jesus as the Way, the Truth, and the Life will find their names written on the door of a room in the Father's house. There is no other Savior and, consequently, no other faith but that which trusts Jesus for salvation.

Remember also how the Father works this faith, through Word and sacrament. At my baptism he softened my stony heart of unbelief and made it into a bed for the Christ Child. Through the years of my life, he has been at work, often silent and unnoticed, on my heart as I listened to the Word and grew in the faith. In the Holy Supper, he assures me again and again for the strengthening of my faith that his Son gave his body and shed his blood, not just for a world of sinners but for me! My confession of faith in Christ, just as did Peter's, comes as a blessing from a gracious Father in heaven. Whatever "rock" I might be is his gift.

Whenever Peter forgot this, he ran into trouble. So do we. Peter, at least till Christ's ascension, could turn to the living Word for assurance of the truth and strength for his faith. So can we. For whenever we turn to the written Word, we see Jesus before us just as real as he stood that day before Peter and the other disciples. Trusting in him through the Word is not venturing out on thin ice. It's standing on the only sure foundation there is!

Prayer: How blessed we are to know you as "the Christ, the Son of the living God," our Savior! Lead us ever more deeply into your Holy Word so that we may see you more clearly, trust you more closely, and confess you more courageously. In life and death, let our prayer be "On Christ, the solid rock, I stand; all other ground is sinking sand." Amen.

St. Timothy, Pastor and Confessor (January 24)

I thank God ... as night and day I constantly remember you in my prayers. I have been reminded of your sincere faith, which first lived in your grandmother Lois and in your mother Eunice and, I am persuaded, now lives in you also. For this reason I remind you to fan into flame the gift of God, which is in you through the laying on of my hands. For God did not give us a spirit of timidity, but a spirit of power, of love and of self-discipline. (2 Timothy 1:3,5-7)

Time to Say Thank You

Often forgotten, seldom spoken are those two little words, *Thank you.* In special needs and on special occasions we remember. Otherwise, we go whistling on our way.

In his last letter from that prison cell in Rome, Paul takes time to say thank you to a gracious God. May Paul's inspired words remind us to do the same and for some of the same reasons.

For faithful parents

What kinds of parents did or do you have? A father who balanced you wobbling on a bicycle seat or trained you in dribbling on a basketball court? A mother who laid her work aside and always had time to listen to your heart? Parents whose loving care and concern, ongoing perspiration, and personal sacrifices provided what you needed and more? If so, then it's time to say thank you to them. And even more so to say thank you to God for them.

Thank God, many of us have more reason to say thank you for faithful parents. If we had a mother and grandmother such as Timothy had in Eunice and Lois, if we had a father such as Timothy had in his "foster father" Paul, then there's special reason for us to voice our thank you to God.

What greater gift can our heavenly Father send our way than parents who held us in their arms at the baptismal font and on their laps in the church benches. Parents who taught our childish hearts simple passages and who folded our pudgy fingers in simple prayers. Parents who reviewed and reinforced for our growing hearts the truths taught us in those confirmation classes and whom we could ask those perplexing teenage questions. Parents who modeled their faith, matching their words with their actions in daily conversation and conduct. If those are the kinds of parents God gave us, then the annual Mother's Day and Father's Day are far too infrequent occasions for saying thank you. Daily let's thank a gracious God for such faith-filled and faithful parents. And if now we are parents ourselves, let's ask God to make us more like them.

For faithful pastors

In a special way, Paul was a "foster father" to Timothy. He took the young believer under his tutelage in a traveling seminary, training him in the truths of God's Word. Even now from that prison cell in Rome, Paul "pastors" Timothy, urging this young coworker to "fan into flame the gift of God." Timothy had received a gift from God that is not given to every believer. From a gracious God had come the ability and the call to serve as a spiritual shepherd of others. Paul urges Timothy to appreciate this gift and put it fully to use. Like blowing on the tiny flame heads in a fledgling campfire, Timothy was to fan God's gift to him, growing in his ministry by immersing himself in God's Word. Through the Word, the Spirit would give Timothy the power to speak boldly, love sacrificially, and labor wisely in his special work of shepherding souls.

What kinds of pastors have we had? Or, if we were so fortunate, what kinds of parochial school teachers? My second-grade teacher inspired in me a love for reading that continues to this day. She also, though I didn't recognize it at the time, planted in me the seed of the desire to become a pastor. Years later she moved to a nursing home near the parish I was serving. After my first visit with her, she wrote me a little note. It began with "thanks to God" for all the pastors she had had and then a "special thanks" for making one of her students into a pastor who could now serve her.

That made me think! When, if ever, had I said thank you to her for teaching me? Even more important, how often had I said thank you to God for sending her? How about you, dear reader? Those who preach and teach today have no easy task. Not only does the unbelieving world send missiles streaking after them, so, at times, do some of the church members. Waning interest in the Word, increased criticism of their actions, resistance to their preaching of the law and the call to repentance, and unreasonable demands on their time and ministry can tempt God's workers to timidity. The result can be diminished boldness, decreased love, and deteriorated self-discipline for the shepherd and equally serious damage for the sheep.

It's better by far to remember God's servants in our prayers, asking that he help them "fan the flame" as Paul did for Pastor Timothy. It's far better to say thank you to them and even more so to a gracious God who has sent them. Nor let us forget our fervent petitions asking God to give us more workers like them and then rolling up our sleeves for the work of recruiting their future replacements from among our own families and our wider church families.

Thank you—two words that are easy to say, but hard to remember. God help us take time to say them.

Prayer: Gracious Lord, thank you for the faith-filled and faithful leaders you have given us in our earthly families and our church family. Open our hearts to treasure the gifts you offer us through them and our lips to speak our thanks to you for them. In Jesus' name. Amen.

The Conversion of St. Paul   (January 25)

Meanwhile, Saul was still breathing out murderous threats against the Lord's disciples. . . . As he neared Damascus on his journey, suddenly a light from heaven flashed around him. He fell to the ground and heard a voice say to him, "Saul, Saul, why do you persecute me?"

"Who are you, Lord?" Saul asked.

"I am Jesus, whom you are persecuting," he replied. "Now get up and go into the city, and you will be told what you must do." (Acts 9:1,3-6)

Good That It Is True!

Too good to be true? Better be careful. When something seems too good to be true, it usually isn't true. How different with the grace of God. Behind the amazing conversion of St. Paul stands the even more amazing grace of God. Behind our conversions too.

Confronted and converted

Who would have guessed the outcome of Saul's trek to Damascus? Not the persecutor nor the ones he was persecuting, never in a million years. When Saul's vicious persecution sent the Christians scattering from Jerusalem, they didn't leave their faith behind. As they moved northeast to Damascus, they carried the message of Jesus with them. As a result, their number expanded instead of becoming eradicated. And Saul in his relentless zeal mounted up to go after them.

Make no mistake about it; his zeal was very real. The followers of that "worthless Galilean" represented the opposite of what Saul believed. Free salvation through a Jesus who had died and rose again collided head-on with salvation earned by the deeds of the law. For Saul the

Pharisee, the gospel was an enemy to which he would give no quarter. That's why "still breathing out murderous threats against the Lord's disciples," he marched to Damascus.

On the final day of that weeklong journey, a light that made the noonday sun seem like darkness flashed down from heaven on Saul. Then followed a voice like none he had ever heard before, calling out to him in judgment and grace. Saul was scratching in the dust, shivering before the One whom he hated vehemently and whose followers he persecuted mercilessly. Can we even imagine what was going on in Saul's mind when the Savior confronted him in such a striking way that day?

We need not imagine what was happening in Saul's heart. Saul the persecutor was converted into Paul the believer. The Lord pulverized Saul's stony heart and planted faith in it. From that day forward, Paul knew himself as the chief of sinners and Jesus as the Savior of sinners—all by God's amazing grace. Do we wonder why Paul used the word *grace* over one hundred times in his letters? For him there was no greater theme than what God's grace had done for him.

When's the last time we stopped to think about our conversion and God's amazing grace behind it? For us it wasn't some bright light and commanding voice from heaven, as it was for Paul. For most of us, it was a seemingly insignificant event at some baptismal font. For some of us, it was seemingly ordinary words about Jesus spoken by a spouse, a neighbor, a pastor. But the miracle was the same.

Though the circumstances behind our conversions were different, our hearts weren't. Like Saul's, they were enemies of God and what he stood for. Like Saul's, they didn't know and didn't want Jesus. Like Saul's, they were resistant and powerless to change till Christ confronted us, as he did Saul on that Damascus road, and put the sign of his cross on our hearts and made them his very own. Now, with Paul, our theme is God's grace and how good it is.

Commissioned and committed

Christ put the sign of the cross not only on Saul's heart that day but also on his life. "You will be told what you must do," he said to the former Pharisee. Acts chapter 26, where Paul retells the story of his conversion, details the commission Christ gave him: "I am sending you to them to open their eyes and turn them from darkness to light, and from the power of Satan to God, so that they may receive forgiveness of sins and a place among those who are sanctified by faith in me" (verses 17,18). Saul was used to giving orders; Paul would get used to receiving them. And that's normal for a Christian. A follower of Christ is someone who stops doing what he or she wants to do and starts doing what Jesus wants him or her to do.

Jesus had huge plans for Paul. From this shapeless, worthless lump of clay, he molded the great apostle to the Gentiles. From that Damascus road, the Savior sent his chosen servant out to the known roads of the world to tell others. The countries Paul visited and the mission congregations he founded, the missionaries he recruited and the souls he led to the great Shepherd are a matter of divine record. For Paul no hill was too high to climb, no sea too wide to cross, no obstacle too heavy to push out of the way, no suffering too severe to slow him down. And behind it all was the amazing grace of Christ. As Paul himself put it, inspired by the Holy Spirit: "If anyone is in Christ, he is a new creation; the old has gone, the new has come! All this is from God, who reconciled us to himself through Christ and gave us the ministry of reconciliation" (2 Corinthians 5:17,18).

"O.H.M.S." was printed on every piece of mail we received from the Canadian government when we were serving the first mission of our synod in that land. We didn't really have to think too long as to what those four initials meant—On Her Majesty's Service. When Jesus puts the sign of the cross on our hearts, he at the same time sends us out On His Majesty's Service. For some of us, it's full-time ministry with the Word. For others it's relating and reflecting that Word as we serve in the homes and neighborhoods, the shops and the stores, the classrooms and the congregations, wherever he places us, with whatever talents he gives us. Nor need we think too long about whether we serve or not. The thought of God's amazing grace will fill us for the task.

Too good to be true? Not when it comes to God's grace and what it did and does for us. Till eternity let our thankful thought be "Good that it is true!"

Prayer: Gracious Lord, how totally undeserved are your gifts of the Savior and our faith to trust in him. Instill in us a deep appreciation for the heaven you have prepared for us through Christ and grateful determination to serve you by spreading the news of salvation however, wherever, and to whomever we can. In your grace watch over us till in heaven we praise you face-to-face. In Jesus' name we ask it. Amen.

St. Titus, Pastor and Confessor

"Therefore, I declare to you today that I am innocent of the blood of all men. For I have not hesitated to proclaim to you the whole will of God. Keep watch over yourselves and all the flock of which the Holy Spirit has made you overseers. Be shepherds of the church of God, which he bought with his own blood." (Acts 20:26-28)

Keep Sending Them, Lord

How often do we think about the called workers God has given us? We get used to having pastors who preach, teachers who teach, staff ministers who guide. When one of them leaves because of another call or other circumstances, we start thinking. Where will we find a replacement? How? What should we expect him or her to do? What qualities should we look for?

Titus, whose festival we are observing, is not mentioned in the verses above. For that matter, he's not mentioned at all in the book of Acts, only in three of Paul's epistles. Yet this servant of God who was converted by Paul, called to serve on the island of Crete, and carried out his ministry faithfully exemplifies the kinds of servants we pray God will keep sending us. What kind might that be? Let's listen as Paul tells the called workers of the church in Ephesus.

Servants who treasure God's flock

"[Guard] all the flock of which the Holy Spirit has made you overseers. Be shepherds of the church of God, which he bought with his own blood," was Paul's earnest command to the workers at Ephesus. Those leaders were to be servants who had the right view of the people whom the Holy Spirit had sent them to serve. "Flock" makes us think of sheep, something many of us know little about. Sheep are trusting creatures, following and depending on their shepherd. A shepherd gains their trust by caring for them and being committed to their well-being.

If that's how shepherds view their sheep, how much more so should called shepherds of God's flock view those under their spiritual care. Every one of them was "bought with his own blood," the blood of God himself. What a striking statement! The purchase price for the church was the very blood of God himself. When Jesus' blood flowed on Calvary, it was the blood of God himself. For what Jesus—true man—was doing, Jesus—true God—was also doing. Precious beyond measure, purchased with divine gold, that's how spiritual shepherds are to value "all the flock," every single one of them, without exception.

The prayer's in order, isn't it? Please, Lord, keep sending us pastors, teachers, staff ministers who treasure your flock. Who value all of us, not just the important and influential, the friendly and the favorable. Who look at us and see not just our sins and shortcomings, though admittedly we have plenty of those, but who ache and long to comfort us with the sweet news of God's own blood shed for us. Who look at our children not as objects to teach or problems to tackle but as lambs of the Savior himself. Who look at their work not only as a job or profession but as a calling you have extended to them. Keep sending such shepherds to us, and we promise we will treasure them too, valuing them as gifts from your gracious hand and viewing their work among us as a rich blessing from you.

Servants who teach God's Word

"I am innocent of the blood of all men. For I have not hesitated to proclaim to you the whole will of God," Paul also reminded the workers in Ephesus. What an example and encouragement for their ministry. For three years Paul had worked in Ephesus, teaching, preaching, admonishing, comforting, his efforts even, as he put it elsewhere, to the point of tears.

Why did Paul labor so strenuously in their midst? He didn't want "blood" on his hands. This time with *blood* he refers not to the precious blood of the God-man, but the blood of the souls for which the Savior died. He didn't want a single person on judgment day to point the finger at him and say, "It's all your fault, Paul, because of what you did or didn't tell me." That's why the apostle worked overtime to "proclaim the whole will of God" to them. What he meant with this phrase he explained earlier in Acts 20:21, "I have declared to both Jews and Greeks that they must turn to God in repentance and have faith in our Lord Jesus." That sentence wraps up all the Bible's teaching. It includes the law in all its severity and the gospel in all its sweetness. It reminds us also that the heart and center of Bible lore is the salvation prepared by God for us through Jesus Christ. Around that blessed teaching revolve all the other teachings. To attack or subtract from any teaching of Scripture is to chip away at the rock of our salvation. To proclaim more or less can only bring damage to precious souls.

Again the prayer's in order, isn't it? Please, Lord, keep sending us pastors, teachers, staff ministers who teach your Word. Who boldly present not what we want to hear, but what we need to hear. Who don't sway with the winds of the times or seek to offer that which sells, but skillfully lay the unchanging truths of your law and gospel before us. Who painfully recognize their own sins and shortcomings before attempting to point out ours. Who kneel at the foot of your cross before they call to us to kneel there. Who immerse themselves in your Word before they attempt to plunge us into it. To whom we can point on judgment day and say, "Thank you, Lord, for sending them to proclaim your Word to us."

How often do we think about the called workers God has given us? Probably not often enough. How often should we pray, "Keep sending them, Lord"? We know the answer.

Prayer: Preserve this ministry while harvest days are keeping;
And since the fields are ripe and hands are few for
       reaping,
Send workers forth, O Lord, the sheaves to gather in
That not a soul be lost which you have come to win.
Amen. (*Christian Worship* [CW] 546:3)

The Presentation of Our Lord (February 2)

When the parents brought in the child Jesus to do for him what the custom of the Law required, Simeon took him in his arms and praised God, saying:

> *"Sovereign Lord, as you have promised,*
> *you now dismiss your servant in peace.*
> *For my eyes have seen your salvation,*
> *which you have prepared in the sight of all people,*
> *a light for revelation to the Gentiles*
> *and for glory to your people Israel."*

There was also a prophetess, Anna. . . . Coming up to them at that very moment, she gave thanks to God and spoke about the child to all who were looking forward to the redemption of Jerusalem. (Luke 2:27-32,36,38)

When Jesus Is Presented

What strikes us in the scene before us? The Old Testament regulations that Mary and Joseph were fulfilling in presenting their 40-day-old baby to the Lord? The Old Testament believers, Simeon and Anna, who approached Mary and Joseph? Or the One at the center of it all?

That's Jesus in Mary's arms. That's Jesus in Simeon's song. That's Jesus in Anna's heart and in her praise. Jesus the Savior. Jesus the only Savior. He was presented that day in the temple; he's still presented today. And when he is, marvelous results still happen.

Possession

We don't know much about Simeon, either his age or occupation. He appears that day in the temple and then

21

disappears, never to be heard from again. But we do know what God had worked in Simeon's heart. Here is a believer who trusted God's promises of the Savior to come. We do know also that God had given Simeon a special promise. His eyes would not close in death till they had actually seen the promised Savior in person.

Then came the day. The Spirit led this Old Testament believer to the temple and right up to that humble Galilean couple. What a scene followed. Simeon, who to this point had the Savior in his heart, now actually held him in his arms. What a gift from the Spirit that Simeon recognized in that lowly little baby, "the Mighty God and Everlasting Father," "the King of kings and Lord of lords." When the Savior was presented that day in the temple, by the Spirit's working Simeon possessed him in his arms and in his heart.

Do you want to hold the Savior? No, not like Simeon, feeling Jesus' little heart beating against your chest, but like Simeon, in your heart of faith, trusting in the Savior? Then you need to turn to the gospel in Word and sacrament. That's the way the Savior comes to people today. Through the Word, in the baptismal font, at the Communion table, the only Savior of the world is still presented to people. Through those marvelous means of grace, the Spirit still works in human hearts. Those who would know Jesus more fully, hold him in their hearts more deeply, fold him to their chests more tightly, turn ever more frequently to those gospel power tools of the Holy Spirit.

Peace

When Jesus is presented, a second blessing follows. We don't know what happened to Simeon after that day in the temple, where he went or how long he lived. But we do know what was in his heart and life. "Peace" is the word he used to describe it, one word, but oh, how much is packed into it. Only those whose sins trouble them can begin to appreciate the peace that follows from hearing their Lord and judge tell them, "The blood of Jesus, my Son, has cleansed you from all your sins." Only those who recognize death as the wage of sin can begin to appreciate the peace that follows from hearing their Lord and judge tell them, "My Son has wiped out death by paying its wage himself and has brought instead life and immortality." To put it another way, only those who by God's grace possess the Savior have a peace that sustains in life and supports in death. Like Simeon they can face each day with the prayer, "Lord, now dismiss your servant in peace."

One day an aged pastor was dictating a letter to the only other remaining member of his seminary class. He told his wife, "Write, 'I am leaving the land of the living and will soon be with the dying.'" But then he hesitated. "No," he said, "change that to 'I am leaving the land of the dying and will soon be with the living.'" Like Simeon he had it right. So do we when we hold the Christ Child in our hearts and trust him to hold us in his arms throughout eternity.

Proclamation

Who should come upon the scene that day when Jesus was presented in the temple but faithful Anna. Many a year, night and day, this widowed believer had spent in the temple, waiting and praying for just such a moment. Read carefully, though. Notice her reaction. She not only gave thanks to God for the Savior she could see and hold. She also "spoke about the child to all who were looking forward to the redemption of Jerusalem." To have is to share. And Anna well understood that truth as she became the first in a long line of women who witnessed about their Savior. Who knows how many ended up holding the Savior as she did because of the blessed news she shared.

What will it look like in heaven someday? Who will be in the number on Jesus' right hand because of the blessed news we shared? No, we can't bring to or keep a single soul in faith in Jesus. That's the Holy Spirit's work. But he would use us to proclaim the gospel through which he works. He would use us to touch our families and friends, our next-door neighbors and utter strangers with the blessed news of a redemption that belongs not just to Jerusalem but to the world. And when we present Jesus, we can expect marvelous things to happen.

Prayer: Heavenly Father, thank you for giving your Son to be the Savior. Thank you for bringing him into our hearts as you did for Simeon and Anna so long ago. Fill our hearts with the joy of his forgiveness and true peace for living and dying. Use us to shine with the light of his salvation out into a sin-darkened world, that others might know the peace that never ends but reaches its fullness in heaven. In his name we ask it. Amen.

St. Matthias, Apostle (February 24)

"For," said Peter, "it is written in the book of Psalms, . . .

" 'May another take his place of leadership.'

Therefore it is necessary to choose one of the men who have been with us the whole time the Lord Jesus went in and out among us, beginning from John's baptism to the time when Jesus was taken up from us. For one of these must become a witness with us of his resurrection."

So they proposed two men: Joseph called Barsabbas (also known as Justus) and Matthias. Then they prayed, "Lord, you know everyone's heart. Show us which of these two you have chosen to take over this apostolic ministry, which Judas left to go where he belongs." Then they cast lots, and the lot fell to Matthias; so he was added to the eleven apostles. (Acts 1:20-26)

Matthias, Messenger of Christ

For almost three years there were 12 of them. Then one was gone, shamefully, sinfully, eternally. A replacement was needed, even required. For God's inspired Word had indicated that another was to take Judas' "place of leadership" (Psalm 109:8). Also, their master, who had chosen 12, had promised that in eternity 12 of them would sit on thrones with him judging the 12 tribes of Israel (Matthew 19:28). Sometime between Christ's ascension and Pentecost, the apostles called the believers in Jerusalem together to choose a replacement for Judas. Even though we no longer have the position of apostle today, how those early followers of Christ went about replacing Judas can teach us much.

Selected by Christ

The unique position of apostle required unique credentials. Only someone who had walked and talked with Jesus from the time of his baptism in the Jordan to his ascension on the Mount of Olives would qualify. Why such requirements? Obviously, more was involved than just having been at Jesus' side and knowing certain facts about him. The candidate was to know Jesus, not just know about him. Rich instruction from the master coupled with faith in him as the Savior were the benchmarks for one who would be selected as an apostle.

Only two candidates were identified, probably from the wider circle of the 70 disciples. Now, how to make the choice between the two? Wisely, the early church left that up to the ascended Lord, who had selected his original twelve. "Lord," they prayed, "show us which of these two you have chosen." Confident that the head of the church had already made his choice and would show it to them, they turned to a method that would allow this to happen. "They cast lots," it says. Whether this meant writing the two names on small pebbles and waiting to see which would pop out of a shaken container or whether it was casting a vote isn't all that important. What strikes us is their confidence in the Lord to indicate his choice in whatever method was used.

We don't have apostles today, but we do have other forms of ministry. Christ has given the church the freedom to choose whatever forms it needs to carry out its task of preaching the gospel. For us at present, those forms include pastors, teachers, and staff ministers. Just as Christ has not dictated the forms of ministry, so he has not prescribed the selection process either. In the case of Matthias, the church cast lots; today we use what is called the divine call process. District presidents present qualified names for church assemblies to vote on, and the selection is made. But always with much prayer and with the confidence that behind it all the Lord is choosing. Whatever process we use must always leave more than enough room for the Lord to show us which one he has chosen. Then those who are called to work and those among whom they work can go forward with confidence regardless of what circumstance might arise.

Nor let us forget the qualifications. We want workers who know Jesus, having been instructed richly in his Word and trusting firmly in him as their Savior. It's not enough for them to say, "Jesus is the Savior" or "Jesus is your Savior." It needs to be first of all, "Jesus is my Savior," for then they'll stand on their heads to teach us about him.

Speaking of Christ

"One of these must become a witness with us of his resurrection," Peter reminded the believers. A witness is not just someone who has seen something, but someone who then tells what he has seen and heard. Why center on the resurrection? Read the book of Acts and the epistles and note how often the resurrection comes up. For the early church the resurrection was the ultimate proof that Jesus is the Savior. The Bethlehem manger standing alone is but a pretty trifle. Add the Calvary cross, but still standing alone, and you have only senseless tragedy. Finish with the empty tomb, and you have glorious triumph. "Born," and "crucified, died, and buried" mean salvation only when completed with those triumphant words, "On the third day he rose again." The emptied tomb says of sin's payment, "done," of heaven's door, "opened," and of the road there, "built."

We hear nothing more of Matthias, where he went or what he did with the message of the resurrection. He's never mentioned again. But why should we wonder? We know what Matthias' message was and what happens when that message is spread. Others are brought to know Jesus and to share in his resurrection. What do we want to hear from our called workers? Don't take the answer to that question for granted. The world around us, perhaps more than ever before, has all kinds of notions as to what it wants to hear. But we know what truly counts. "Take us to his manger bed, take us to his rough cross, but above all take us to his empty tomb," let's demand of those whom the head of the church sends to us. And then let's join them in spreading that message. Not just Matthias, not just our present-day called workers, but all who have been with Jesus are to be messengers of the risen Savior.

Prayer: Lord Jesus, head of the church, thank you for your birth, death, and resurrection in payment for our sins and for those you have sent through the ages to preach that good news to us. Continue to bless us, we ask, by sending workers who truly know you and whose heart's desire is to be witnesses of you, the only Savior. Help us join our efforts with theirs so that the message of your resurrection may spread and more may join us at your side. In your name we ask it. Amen.

When they had gone, an angel of the Lord appeared to Joseph in a dream. "Get up," he said, "take the child and his mother and escape to Egypt. Stay there until I tell you, for Herod is going to search for the child to kill him."

So he got up, took the child and his mother during the night and left for Egypt, where he stayed until the death of Herod. And so was fulfilled what the Lord had said through the prophet: "Out of Egypt I called my son." (Matthew 2:13-15)

More Like Joseph

They didn't even miss him. Shortly before the Christmas Eve service began, Billy's mom called the church office to report him as ill. It was too late to find a replacement. As a result the role he was supposed to play was dropped. And no one commented on the fact that there was no Joseph in the Christmas scene.

Yet we don't want to miss Joseph. There's much that we can learn from him, and as we do, we find ourselves praying, "Lord, make us more like Joseph."

An ordinary man

The Magi had come and gone. Warned by God, they headed home by a different route, but with the treasured Savior they had come seeking. Outwitted by the Magi, Herod lashed out. Quaking on his throne because of a baby, he ordered the massacre of the baby boys in Bethlehem. And in their number would have been the baby Jesus if it had not been for Joseph.

While the Magi were heading home and Herod was hatching his devilish plot, an angel of the Lord came to Joseph. "Take the child and his mother and escape to Egypt. Stay there until I tell you," was the command. Nor did the angel have to repeat it. There was no "Why leave the country? Can't we go to Nazareth instead?" No "How long did you say we would have to stay?" Instead, the lowly, almost invisible, carpenter from Nazareth that very night bundled up his bride and baby boy and left for Egypt.

Do you begin to see the reason for the prayer "Lord, make us more like Joseph"? He simply trusted whatever God told him and humbly obeyed whatever God asked of him. He knew the baby in Mary's womb wasn't his; no one knew that better than he did. Yet he took Mary as his wife and Jesus as his foster son because God told him to. He was ready to head home to his carpenter's shop in Nazareth to make a living for his little family. Yet he didn't hesitate to go in the opposite direction to a strange land for who knew how long because God told him to. Scripture records not a single one of his words. Yet from this ordinary person standing in the background of the wondrous story of our salvation comes an example of humble trust in God's promises and willing obedience to God's commands.

Has God ever asked us to walk on ways far different than we might choose? Only to have our faith stub its toe and stumble on the path of obedience instead of striding briskly forward? Has it ever happened that we hesitated and even refused to believe one or more of God's promises because they seemed impossible? Then let's remember Joseph, the ordinary man. We don't have any of his words recorded, but we do know that he listened to God's words. Therein lay his strength and ours too. The more we listen to God's promises, like Joseph, the more will come strength to trust and follow.

A more than ordinary child

Joseph was an ordinary man, but to him God gave a position of utmost importance. He was to care for God's Son, that little baby upon whom the salvation of the world depended. It's on that Christ Child that we need to focus, just as Joseph did.

There had been no room in the inn for the promised Savior; now there wasn't even room in the Promised Land. When he fled to Egypt, which was the country remembered by his people as a land of slavery and oppression, it was a portent of things to come. Humiliation and rejection would follow, even pursue him, and not cease till the cross claimed him. But in all of this there was a divine purpose. Through the life and death of his Son, a gracious Father in heaven was fulfilling the salvation of the world, which he had already planned in eternity. The banishment of the baby Jesus from Canaan to Egypt was part of God's divine plan that would result in our dwelling forever in the Canaan above.

The flight to Egypt was also fulfillment of an Old Testament prophecy. In Hosea 11:1 God was referring first of all to the Israelites as his son, languishing in slavery in Egypt, with the words "Out of Egypt I called my son." Now the Holy Spirit, who inspired those words, applies them also to the Christ Child, God's own Son from all eternity. From Egypt God would call his Son, just as he did Israel years earlier, to carry his saving name out into the world. God called the Israelites home to Canaan so that the Christ Child could be born of them. God would call his Son, Jesus, out of Egypt so that he could walk the way of salvation to the filled cross and emptied grave, not just for Israel but for the world.

Wouldn't it be something if we could have been in Joseph's place? If God would have entrusted that marvelous, far more than ordinary Christ Child into our care? In a sense, that's exactly what he has done by placing into our hands the message of the only name under heaven by which we must be saved. Doesn't that thought bring us again to the prayer "Lord, make us more like Joseph"? Teach us to treasure what you have given us in Christ Jesus and then lead us to respond by carrying this only Savior out into a world that so desperately needs him.

No, we don't want to miss Joseph. Even more so do we not want to miss Jesus.

Prayer: Gracious Lord, Father of Jesus and through him our Father, accept the thanks we bring for the Savior you have sent and the promises of salvation and life we have through him. Fasten our eyes, like Joseph's, on your promises so that our trust in the Savior may increase and our desire to serve him flourish. Help us use our lives wherever you have placed us to carry your Son, our Savior, to the world. In his name we ask it. Amen.

But the angel said to her, "Do not be afraid, Mary, you have found favor with God. You will be with child and give birth to a son, and you are to give him the name Jesus."

"How will this be," Mary asked the angel, "since I am a virgin?"

The angel answered, "The Holy Spirit will come upon you, and the power of the Most High will overshadow you. So the holy one to be born will be called the Son of God."

"I am the Lord's servant," Mary answered. "May it be to me as you have said." Then the angel left her. (Luke 1:30,31,34,35,38)

What If the Angel Had Come to Us?

Count ahead nine months from March 25, and see where you land. Back in the fifth century the church started celebrating the angel's announcement to Mary that she was to be the mother of the Christ Child and pegged the date at March 25. This poses the question, doesn't it? What if we were to shift our Christmas celebration from December 25 to March 25? Let the world have the tinsel and the trappings with which it surrounds and almost suffocates that December day, while we go back to what it's all about. And that poses another question. What is Christmas really all about? Let's try to answer by asking still another question. What if the angel who announced the Savior's conception to Mary had come to us? What would our reactions be?

Somewhat afraid?

Mary was afraid. The angel who had come to announce her pregnancy even had to tell her, "Do not be afraid." Unmarried pregnant women did not have an easy time in her day. Besides the shame and gossip, she had to face the laws of the land, which stated that an adulteress could be stoned to death. Also what about Joseph? What would his reaction be to her carrying a baby that he knew was not his? Mary was afraid for an even greater reason. Not only can sinful man not stand in the presence of a holy God, he cannot even face one of God's holy angels. Like the shepherds later on the plains of Bethlehem and the three disciples on the Mount of Transfiguration, Mary had a holy fear because of her sins.

Can we put ourselves into Mary's shoes? I hope so. The celebration of Christmas can't be very real if there's no fear in our hearts. The Christ Child in the manger won't mean much to us if we don't take time to reexamine the reason for his coming. And it's the cause for his coming that ought to make us afraid. When we pull back the paper-thin veneer of respectability we like to glue over our hearts, what do we see? Is it a "bed, soft, undefiled, a quiet chamber kept for the Christ Child"? Or a roiling reservoir awash with sin? We know the answer. Just a brief review of a handful of our thoughts, words, and deeds each day causes us to turn our faces aside before a just and holy God, just as Mary did before his angelic messenger.

Very much amazed?

Mary was amazed. The miracle of God's favor or grace that had selected her, all unworthy though she was, was beyond comprehension. Add to that the news that she was to be pregnant with God's divine Son, the Savior long promised since sin had closed Eden's door, and her amazement meter must have skyrocketed. Then too there was her practical question, which received a more than amazing answer. She who was still a virgin was to be pregnant by the miraculous working of the Holy Spirit. Her baby would be "the holy one" with no sinful heart inherited from a set of sinful parents. He would also be God's gift, the incredible miracle of God's infinite love taking on the finite shape of true man, all to save a sinful race from its sins.

Can we put ourselves into Mary's shoes, asking our own questions of amazement? "How will this be?" we ask when our sins, both old ones, into which we slip so speedily and new ones, which sneak up on us so stealthily, are declared washed away by Jesus' blood. "How will this be?" we ask when feeling abandoned and adrift on life's seas, and we see the Lord walking toward us on top of the waves. "How will this be?" we ask when mourning loved ones left beneath the grave's fresh mound or moving relentlessly toward that mound ourselves, and we hear the risen Savior say, "Because I live, you also will live." The answer is still the same. What the angel told Mary applies to us too, "for nothing is impossible" with the Lord. Pray God our reaction may be the same—the amazement of faith, which trusts God's sure promises.

Willingly obedient?

Mary was obedient. "I am the Lord's servant," she willingly answered. "May it be to me as you have said." Though she couldn't understand, she believed and was willing to follow as God's servants always are. They are not only willing to carry out what he asks but find joy in doing so.

Once more, can we put ourselves into Mary's shoes? When the Lord comes to us with work to be done for him and lives to be lived for him, do we say "I am the Lord's servant"? Whenever we celebrate Christmas (and hopefully that is all year long), do we rise from our Savior's manger bed asking the questions "What do you want, Jesus? What can I do for you?" Christ born in our hearts means also Christ living in our lives. Willing obedience is the best gift we can offer our God any time of the year.

A disobedient child, who had been scolded by his mother, came minutes later running into her arms. Sobbing in repentance, he blurted out, "Momma, I'm sorry. I love you. I love you so much." Sweeping up her child and squeezing him close, the mother replied, "When you do as I say, then I'll know how much you really love me." May God with his amazing grace work in us a willing obedience that shows all year long how much we love him.

What if that angel had come to us? He hasn't, but the Christ Child has!

Prayer: O holy Child of Bethlehem, descend to us, we pray;
Cast out our sin and enter in; be born in us today.
We hear the Christmas angels the great glad tidings tell;
Oh, come to us, abide with us, our Lord Immanuel!
Amen. (CW 65:4)

St. Mark, Evangelist   (April 25)

After John was put in prison, Jesus went into Galilee, proclaiming the good news of God. "The time has come," he said. "The kingdom of God is near. Repent and believe the good news!"

As Jesus walked beside the Sea of Galilee, he saw Simon and his brother Andrew casting a net into the lake, for they were fishermen. "Come, follow me," Jesus said, "and I will make you fishers of men." At once they left their nets and followed him. (Mark 1:14-18)

What Does Jesus Have to Say?

Remember John Mark? Probably not. He was not one of the Twelve. Nor was the spotlight directly on him. This convert of Peter, cousin of Barnabas, and work companion of both Paul and Peter stood in the shadows. Yet the Holy Spirit selected him to pen one of the books of the New Testament. What does Mark have to say in the gospel that bears his name? Nothing about himself, but much about Jesus, his Savior and ours. Let's listen to Jesus as Mark records him speaking also to us.

"Repent and believe the good news"

Some time has elapsed since Jesus began his ministry with his baptism by John and his temptation by the devil. In a prison cell, John the Baptist's voice is now muffled, but to the north in Galilee, Jesus' voice is picking up in volume. "The kingdom of God is near," the Savior proclaims. "Repent and believe the good news," he urges.

That's not what some thought he should be saying. To the Pharisees words about repentance were disquieting and discomforting. They preferred words of praise polishing their outward image, not arrows of repentance penetrating to their rotten core. To Israel's national leaders, Christ's words were just as distasteful. Much rather would they have heard words about rallying around the flag and rebelling against Rome's hated legions instead of talk about the heavenly kingdom and how to prepare for it. No wonder they turned away from Jesus, then turned against him, later even rushed him to the cross.

Sound somewhat familiar? To some, Christ's words about repentance still are far too demanding. Their ears prefer a mellower message, one that tunes out or at least tones down condemnation of "in vogue" sins like selfish abortion, sinful divorce, or sexual promiscuity. As always, there are preachers willing to oblige them so that the sinner can still feel somewhat religious. To others, Christ's words about the kingdom of God are too moldy and moth-eaten to appeal to a 21st century. Replacing such words is the renewed cry for the church to enter the political arena and to do something for the here and now. And again there are those who obligingly offer such a message.

But the important question still is, "What does Jesus have to say?" His message has not changed since that day long ago in Galilee. It is still that same message of repentance and the good news of the kingdom of God that Mark recorded. That message can still be summed up with four *Rs*: the *realization* that we have sinned, the *regret* that we have sinned against a holy God, the *reliance* on his full forgiveness to cover those sins, and the *resolve* to fight against those sins. Such a message is always up-to-date, regardless of how often we have heard it or in what century we are listening to it.

Certainly we all agree that those outside the church and those living notoriously sinful lives need to hear Jesus' words about repentance. But how about us? Dare it ever become in the church service, "Come on, Pastor, not that same old stuff again"? Or "Go away, Pastor, and leave that pet sin of mine alone"? Or should it rather be again and again, "Please, Pastor, preach those four *R*s. Keep on telling us how Jesus said, 'Repent and believe the good news.'"

"Follow me, and I will make you fishers of men"

The Savior has more to say, as Mark reminds us. In Galilee that day he told Simon and Andrew, later also James and John, "Follow me, and I will make you fishers of men." They obeyed, leaving their fishing tackle and, in the case of the Zebedee brothers, also their father behind. So important did they consider Jesus' words to be.

And what about us? The Savior may not call us to leave jobs and family behind for full-time service in his kingdom. His call to us may be to serve him right where we are with what he has given us. Sometimes I wonder whether that call isn't the hardest form of fishing. Not going off to some distant lake but staying right at home, fishing for souls in the small ponds that we know as our hometowns. Helping with our offerings to build the boats for those who go fishing in our name in the seas of the world. Urging our children, like Zebedee's sons, to prepare for full-time fishing in his kingdom. The kingdom needs not just called workers but committed disciples doing kingdom work quietly and unspectacularly in a million nooks and crannies of the world. The great need is for believers who will do the Lord's thing where and while they are doing their thing in office, shop, and home. The great need is for people like you and me who have heard Jesus say, "Follow me, and I will make you fishers of men."

"Repent and believe." "Follow me and fish." That's what the Savior has to say. Words important enough that the Spirit prompted Mark to record them so that they could ring also in our ears and hearts. God help our actions show that we are listening.

Prayer: Thank you, Lord, for bringing your message of repentance and forgiveness to us again and again. Open our hearts to believe and our lives to respond. Lead us to recognize our sins, regret them deeply, resolve not to repeat them even as we reach for the rich forgiveness your Son has readied for us. Encourage and equip us for the work you have given us, that of fishing for souls. Bless our efforts so that others may stand with us in your heavenly kingdom. Amen.

St. Philip, Apostle (May 1)

The next day Jesus decided to leave for Galilee. Finding Philip, he said to him, "Follow me."

Philip, like Andrew and Peter, was from the town of Bethsaida. Philip found Nathanael and told him, "We have found the one Moses wrote about in the Law, and about whom the prophets also wrote—Jesus of Nazareth, the son of Joseph."

"Nazareth! Can anything good come from there?" Nathanael asked.

"Come and see," said Philip.

When Jesus looked up and saw a great crowd coming toward him, he said to Philip, "Where shall we buy bread for these people to eat?" He asked this only to test him, for he already had in mind what he was going to do.

Philip answered him, "Eight months wages would not buy enough bread for each one to have a bite!" (John 1:43-46; 6:5-7)

Philip, the Disciple Who Was Practical and Yet Not Practical Enough

Don't you admire practical people? Every time I try to use a miter box, the corners of the picture frame never quite seem to fit. But some people can do it right every time. Then there are those who are too practical, like the wanna-be carpenter who measures and remeasures before putting the saw to the board. The apostle Philip was a practical fellow at times and yet at other times not practical enough.

He was practical

All we know about Philip comes from the gospel of John. In the other three gospels we find his name in the listing of the Twelve, but in John's gospel we find his character unfolded. Philip was his name, a Greek word meaning "lover of horses." Bethsaida, a fishing village on the Sea of Galilee, was his home. In the listing of the Twelve he's always in fifth place, perhaps indicating that he was the fifth disciple called by Jesus.

The day Jesus called him was the most practical day in Philip's life. Note that the Savior found him; Philip didn't find the Savior. The master called him; Philip didn't call the master. No more than metal filings can find the magnet do sinners find the Savior. It's always the Good Shepherd's doings and always behind them is the unmerited grace of God. Nothing can be more practical than God's grace, which gives the sinner the most important things he can have, a Savior and faith in the Savior.

Philip would tell us that. Philip could tell us about something else most practical: sharing the Savior with others. Those found by Christ become active in finding others. "We have found him," Philip hurried to tell his friend Nathanael, "the Savior long foretold in the Old Testament is here." When his friend was rather skeptical, Philip had his practical answer ready. "Come and see," he said. "Forget about Nazareth. Come and see for yourself."

Remember that nationwide poll from several years ago? It surveyed those who were "highly spiritually committed" and discovered that such people were much more inclined to be content with their situations in life, their marriages, their friends, and so on. Why not? What can be more practical for our earthly existence than to have Jesus? To have his forgiveness for all our sins, his help for all our troubles, his comfort for all our sorrows, his heaven for our souls has to have an impact on our daily lives also.

For us also, to have Jesus means to share him, like the adult convert who the day before her confirmation came seeking advice about bringing her parents to the Jesus she now had.

Witnessing about Jesus requires neither a course in speech nor a seminary diploma. All that is needed is the conviction that Jesus is the most practical treasure anyone can have. At the end of his hospital visit to a neighbor dying of cancer, the church member asked, "May I say a prayer for you?" "Nah," the neighbor answered, "forget it." Startled, the church member stammered, "Why? Don't you believe in Jesus?" He received the answer, "For 20 years now we have been living next door to each other and you've never once said anything to me about Jesus." Our concern about witnessing to our family, neighbors, friends, acquaintances depends on one practical matter, doesn't it? It depends on how much of a treasure we consider the Savior to be.

He was not practical enough

There came a time, though, when Philip wasn't practical enough. Remember that day out by the lake when the crowd listening to Jesus grew larger and larger and stayed later and later until a problem arose? It was time to eat and too late to send them away. Practical Philip punched a few buttons on his mental calculator and stammered, "We don't have enough money, and even if we did, where would we buy the bread?" Philip had a warm heart but a pessimistic head. He let his common sense get in the way of his trust in Jesus. His practical answer was, "We can't handle it," when an even more practical answer would have been, "But, Lord Jesus, you can," as the Savior showed with the barley loaves and small fishes.

Sound familiar? Do we sometimes have to feel our backs up against the wall with that hospital bed, that funeral home visitation, that problem in our family before we cast an eye in Jesus' direction? Even then, do we sometimes fasten our eyes too much on the problem and too little on the Lord Jesus? Faith doesn't need to ask to see. It trusts the One who all our sorrows shares and to whom we can carry everything in prayer.

Do we want to be practical regardless of how we miter a corner or saw a board? Then let's learn from Philip to keep our eyes on Jesus.

Prayer: On my heart imprint your image,
Blessed Jesus,
King of grace,
That life's riches, cares, and pleasures
Have no power to hide your face.
This the superscription be: Jesus, crucified for me,
Is my life, my hope's foundation,
And my glory and salvation. Amen. (CW 320)

St. James and St. Simon, Apostles   (May 1 & October 28)

And whatever you do, whether in word or deed, do it all in the name of the Lord Jesus, giving thanks to God the Father through him. (Colossians 3:17)

James and Simon, Disciples Who Were Little Known but Well Remembered

From the past comes an interesting legend about the building of a magnificent cathedral. It seems that the angel in charge promised a rare prize to whoever would make the most significant contribution to the building. All wondered whether it would be the architect with his brilliant plans or the stone masons with their special skills or the woodworker with his intricate carvings on the altar. Imagine the surprise when the moment came and the prize was awarded to a peasant woman. Every day without fail she had carried the hay for the oxen that pulled the marble slabs for the stonecutter.

Before us we have two of Christ's twelve disciples from whom we can learn that little things and inconspicuous people are important. From them can come the reminder, just as it came later from the apostle Paul, that we are to use all that we have and do all that we do, whether much or little, for the Lord.

Little known

In all the lists of the disciples in Scripture, he is called James, the son of Alphaeus, but that doesn't tell us much. Mark relates that his mother's name was Mary and that she was among the women at the cross. But again that tells us little except perhaps that James must have won his mother for Christ. Again it is Mark who labels him as James the younger, but we are left guessing as to what that means. In the listing of the disciples, he's down in the ninth spot, down near the bottom.

Of Simon we know even less. We have only his name in the listing of the disciples. Matthew and Mark call him Simon the Canaanite, while Luke in his gospel and in Acts calls him Simon the Zealot. *Canaanite* comes from the Hebrew and means "zealous" or "enthusiastic," while *zealot* comes from the Greek and means the same. Does this indicate that Simon belonged to the fanatical Jewish underground group called the Zealots? We don't know. This much we do know, that he is twice in the 11th place and twice in the 10th place in the four listings of the disciples. Only Judas Iscariot is placed lower than he.

Do you begin to understand why we might label both James and Simon as disciples who were little known?

But well remembered!

Every time the Twelve are named, both James and Simon are remembered. We're remembering them right now, and it's well that we do. For they had the blessed privilege of being with the Lord when he walked visibly on earth. The Savior himself taught them day after day in his traveling seminary. The Savior himself sent them out as vicars on preaching missions. They were with him in the wilderness and saw the loaves and fishes multiply in his hands, giving proof of how he could care for their earthly needs. They were with him in the upper room as he spoke again of his coming death and how it would take care of their souls. They stumbled for a while when his crucifixion came, but after they had seen the risen Jesus, there was no more stumbling and no more turning back.

And having been with Jesus, they just simply had to work for him. Whatever they did in word or deed was for him, their Savior and their Lord. No, we aren't told what they did. Scripture doesn't mention monumental deeds or milestone events with their names attached. But can we be wrong in saying that they lived and worked for him who had done his all for them? Though we know so little about them, yet we do well to remember them as representatives of "Christ's forgotten followers," those nameless millions who over the centuries since have served the Lord quietly and faithfully.

Will our names be remembered and our deeds recorded after the grave has claimed our remains? Does it really matter? After we have lived a few years, we begin to realize how unimportant names really are, except for one, the blessed name of our Savior. We begin to understand also that the important part is that the kingdom work be done, not who does it. Down through the ages God has carried on much of his work through those little people about whom little is known, those "forgotten followers" whose gravestones might read "They did what they could."

So you grandmothers out there, keep on praying. You have so many to pray for, and with the wisdom of your years, you know what to ask. Only pray as hard as you can. You parents out there, keep on parenting. Your children are precious; their souls are eternal. Only parent as hard as you can. You pastors and teachers out there, keep on preaching and teaching. Sometimes you may think your work is in vain, that it's like talking to so many lifeless posts, but keep on as hard as you can, for God has promised that his Word works. You Christian leaders out there, keep on leading in our congregations and circles, but always doing your best with your best. The time for us to work for Jesus will so quickly be past, and we'll go to our graves forgotten. But Jesus' name will be remembered by more—Jesus, the only saving name under heaven. Forgotten followers we may be, but let's not forget one most important truth. Do we realize what we have in our Savior? Do we know what it means to have our sins forgiven and forgotten? to have heaven as our sure home through him? to have a gracious Lord who will see us through anything in life? The more we are reminded of this as we walk with him in his Word, the more we will be not just his forgotten but also his zealous followers.

Prayer: Please, Lord Jesus, draw us into your Holy Word so that we may see you more clearly. Then help us so that whatever we do in word or deed is done in your name and gives thanks to God our Father. Amen.

The Visitation

At that time Mary got ready and hurried to a town in the hill country of Judea, where she entered Zechariah's home and greeted Elizabeth. When Elizabeth heard Mary's greeting, the baby leaped in her womb, and Elizabeth was filled with the Holy Spirit. In a loud voice she exclaimed: "Blessed are you among women, and blessed is the child you will bear! But why am I so favored, that the mother of my Lord should come to me? As soon as the sound of your greeting reached my ears, the baby in my womb leaped for joy. Blessed is she who has believed that what the Lord has said to her will be accomplished!" (Luke 1:39-45)

That's Incredible!

How would we describe the account if we were hearing it for the first time? A young woman is with child, but still a virgin. She comes to break the news to her relative, only to have her relative tell her all about it. That relative also is pregnant, but well beyond the age of childbearing. Her six–month-old unborn baby moves in her womb, not just stirring around, but jumping for joy at what has been said. And most incredible of all, the baby just beginning to form in the young woman's womb is God from all eternity. Yes, what would we have said?

Does the word *incredible* come to mind? For the unbeliever viewing Mary's visit to Elizabeth, the word means "impossible beyond belief." For believers like you and me, it means "beyond our understanding," but nevertheless true because of the amazing power and grace of God.

Incredible news

Mary couldn't wait to get there. The 75-mile trek must have seemed to take forever. What news she had to share with her elderly cousin, Elizabeth! But she didn't even get the chance. For no sooner had she walked through the door and greeted her cousin, than Elizabeth described her as the most blessed among women and spoke of the child in Mary's womb. Nor was that all. Elizabeth also greeted her as "the mother of my Lord."

How did Elizabeth know all this? The answer, simply put, was, "Elizabeth was filled with the Holy Spirit." Not only did the Spirit reveal to her that Mary was with child, but he revealed the even more incredible news that the child carried in Mary's womb and cradled beneath her heart was the Lord himself.

The world snickers and scoffs at the incredible news of God the Eternal counting life in days, of God the Almighty being formed cell by cell, of God the Provider needing nourishment from a mother's blood—and all this in the womb of a virgin. "Incredible," is their response, "impossible, unbelievable." But for us that word means beyond our understanding, yet nevertheless true because of the amazing power and grace of our God.

Incredible joy

Elizabeth was bursting with joy, as both the loudness of her voice and her question indicated. What a favor that "the mother of her Lord" should come to visit her. It's almost as if Elizabeth had been present in the shadows at Nazareth when the angel had announced the Savior's coming birth to Mary. This aged believer knew where the emphasis belonged—on the "blessed child" Mary was carrying. That incredible baby was the Lord come to be her Savior. And that's why Elizabeth rejoiced so mightily.

Her unborn baby also rejoiced by the working of the same Holy Spirit. Three months before entering this world, John rejoiced in the Christ, who had just days before been conceived in Mary's womb. Thirty years later it would be John's job and joy to point out in person the Lamb of God, who had come to take away the sins of the world. Incredible, you say, that an unborn child should rejoice in the coming Savior. Not at all, for this is no greater miracle than the faith and joy the Holy Spirit works in the hearts of our newly born infants through Baptism.

Mary was "blessed" by God's grace to give birth to and share in the Savior. Note that the word *blessed,* not the word *happy,* is used. *Happy* speaks of how we feel; *blessed,* of what we are. *Blessed* also implies an agent, someone who makes us what we are. Have we not also been richly blessed by God's grace? We cannot carry the Christ Child in a womb, but we can carry him in our hearts. We cannot join Elizabeth in talking to Mary about the joy of our salvation, at least not this side of heaven, but we can talk to one another. Let the world describe what God has given us as too incredible to be believed. For us it's a reason for unending joy.

Incredible gift

Mary believed all the incredible things God had told her. Elizabeth pointed this out with the words, "Blessed is she who has believed that what the Lord has said to her will be accomplished." Later Jesus also pointed to Mary's faith (Luke 11:27,28). When an enthusiastic woman interrupted one of his sermons with praise for Mary because of her close contact with Jesus, he set the record straight for all time. Mary was blessed not because she had given birth to and nursed him, but because she heard and believed his words. Otherwise, though favored by God's grace in being chosen to give birth to the Savior, she still would have been lost eternally. Her faith too was an incredible gift from a gracious God.

So how come in a world where more than 75 percent of the people don't know or believe in Jesus as Savior, you and I do? How come our names are written in the book of life in heaven? How come we join Mary, Elizabeth, John the Baptist, and so many others in rejoicing in Jesus already here on earth and looking forward to doing much more of the same in heaven? Where does this faith of ours come from? Let's never forget the answer. It's still all an amazing miracle of divine power and grace. It's still all the incredible gift of God's Holy Spirit.

Prayer: What incredible news you have given us, Lord: the birth of your own Son come to be our Savior. Strengthen the faith you have worked in us so that we believe this news, rejoice greatly because of it, and seek to share it with those around us so that more might join us with Mary, Elizabeth, and John in the unending joys of heaven at the Savior's side. Amen.

St. Barnabas, Apostle   (June 11)

Some of them, however, men from Cyprus and Cyrene, went to Antioch and began to speak to Greeks also, telling them the good news about the Lord Jesus. The Lord's hand was with them, and a great number of people believed and turned to the Lord.

News of this reached the ears of the church at Jerusalem, and they sent Barnabas to Antioch. When he arrived and saw the evidence of the grace of God, he was glad and encouraged them all to remain true to the Lord with all their hearts. He was a good man, full of the Holy Spirit and faith, and a great number of people were brought to the Lord. (Acts 11:20-24)

What Do We Want Our Congregations to Be?

To what kind of congregation do you belong? A big one steeped in years of history or a small one just starting out? One in the Midwest where our synod is well known or one out in the coastal areas where WELS means nothing? One worshiping in an impressive facility or one meeting in temporary quarters?

It doesn't really matter much, does it? The more important question is, What do we want our congregations to be? Let's take a look at the congregation in Antioch, where Barnabas worked, and find some answers.

One growing in God's Word

What did Barnabas find when he arrived in Antioch? News had filtered back to the mother church in Jerusalem about this young congregation, composed of Jewish Christians whom persecution had scattered from Jerusalem and of

Greek converts with whom they had shared their faith in their newfound home. Of course, the mother church was vitally interested. For the congregation at Antioch was the first major attempt at bringing "the good news about the Lord Jesus" to non-Jews. So Barnabas was sent to take a look.

The first thing Barnabas noted was "evidence of the grace of God." He looked beyond the growing number of Christians in Antioch to what had made them such. It was God's grace, his undeserved favor, that had sent the Savior for them and then also the Spirit to bring them to faith in the Savior. What a pastoral heart Barnabas had to note not just the numbers but God's grace behind them.

What else did Barnabas find in the Antioch congregation? Obviously, congregation members who were interested in learning more about their salvation. So Barnabas, aided by Paul, worked in their midst a full year, teaching them and "encourag[ing] them all to remain true to the Lord with all their hearts." Again, what a pastoral heart Barnabas had, one that yearned to lead people even closer to Jesus and that knew how to do it, through patient instruction in God's Word. Also, what a congregation that was, one eager to follow their leader into the Word. As always, the Lord had chosen the right man for this new mission field, big-hearted Barnabas, whose name means "son of encouragement." Also as always, the Lord's blessings followed as these new Christians were fed with the Word.

What would Barnabas find if he were to visit our congregations? Hopefully, Christians who are eager for the Word. Christians who say to their pastor, "Come on, feed us, not just with the minimum calories necessary but with as many as possible in as many ways as possible." Christians whose homes are miniature churches where the Bread of Life is sliced thickly each day for themselves and their families. Christians who want to grow in God's Word, beginning with me!

One going with God's Word

Barnabas found something else in that Antioch congregation. He found believers vitally interested in sharing "the good news about the Lord Jesus." Growing in God's Word oneself and then going with that Word to others are inseparably linked. The more hearts grow in faith and knowledge of the only Savior, the more they yearn to share this treasure.

Those Jewish refugees from Jerusalem had carried God's Word with them, not just so they could still have it, but so they might share it with others. When in Antioch they reached out to others with that saving Word, it was not just to their own kind, but to the Gentiles, something almost unheard of at that time. Jesus died for all, and those who have Jesus reach out to all, regardless of how similar or dissimilar they may be.

What would Barnabas find if he were to visit our congregations? Hopefully, ones that are on fire with desire to go out with God's Word. The sign at the exit from the parking lot of one of our churches in Florida said simply, "You are entering the mission field." What a reminder! Our congregations are not some kind of bunker in which we hunker down for safety but substations to power us for our mission. Just as in Antioch, our congregations are there to help us grow in God's Word so that we might go out with

God's Word. Also just as in Antioch, our communities are increasingly composed of people who are different from us. So what? Souls come in only two kinds. Either they are dirtied by sin's curse and are being consumed by death's gangrene, or they are cleansed and healed by the blood of the Lamb. What we do with God's Word makes the difference! Only the Holy Spirit, as he did in Antioch, can bring sinners to faith, but this he does through "the good news about the Lord Jesus." And that good news he has placed into our hands.

What do we want our congregations to be? Please, Lord, let them be growing in your Word and then going with your Word, beginning with me.

Prayer: Oh, teach us, Lord, that we may teach the precious truths which you impart,
And wing our words that they may reach the hidden depths of many a heart.
Oh, fill us with your fullness, Lord, until our very hearts o'erflow
In kindling thought and glowing word your love to tell, your praise to show. Amen.
(CW 561:3,4)

The Nativity of St. John the Baptist (June 24)

When it was time for Elizabeth to have her baby, she gave birth to a son. Her neighbors and relatives heard that the Lord had shown her great mercy, and they shared her joy.

On the eighth day they came to circumcise the child, and they were going to name him after his father Zechariah, but his mother spoke up and said, "No! He is to be called John."

They said to her, "There is no one among your relatives who has that name."

Then they made signs to his father, to find out what he would like to name the child. He asked for a writing tablet, and to everyone's astonishment he wrote, "His name is John." Immediately his mouth was opened and his tongue was loosed, and he began to speak, praising God. The neighbors were all filled with awe, and throughout the hill country of Judea people were talking about all these things. Everyone who heard this wondered about it, asking, "What then is this child going to be?" For the Lord's hand was with him. (Luke 1:57-66)

"What Then Is This Child Going to Be?"

"What will our child be?" expectant parents wonder as it grows under its mother's heart and later nestles in its mother's arms. More often than not, their parental musings miss the mark. Not so with the newly born child in our account. His aged parents knew exactly what their son was going to be. They even knew what to name him, for an angel of the Lord had told them.

A very special child

For nine months John's father, Zechariah, had been unable to speak because he had not believed the angel's message. "What would you have done?" he might ask, turning to us.

"Would you have believed it? Do you know how many times Elizabeth and I hoped and prayed that she would become pregnant, but nothing happened? Finally, we gave up and accepted the sad fact that we were going to the grave childless. Till that day in the temple when that angel stood suddenly before me with that incredible message from the Lord. We were going to have a baby and his name was to be John. Can you imagine? I couldn't! And because I couldn't, I ended up speechless.

"Till the day of our baby's circumcision. What a special baby he was, a miracle baby, the joy of our life. The whole neighborhood and all of our relatives shared our joy, recognizing the Lord's great mercy. Our house bubbled with laughter and joy. But I couldn't speak. You should have seen Elizabeth. How radiantly happy and supremely thankful to the Lord she was. You also should have heard her when the relatives insisted that our baby be named Zechariah Junior. 'No, he is to be named John,' she said. When they looked in my direction, I knew what to answer. I had learned my lesson. You can always take God at his word regardless of how impossible those words seem. 'John,' I scribbled down on my writing tablet. 'His name is John.' 'What then is this child going to be?' people wondered, but Elizabeth and I knew. He was a special child with a special name, a son entrusted to us by a gracious God."

Every baby conceived is something special, a sign from God that he has not given up on the human race. Though some resent children, viewing them as burdens, God considers each one of them special. Though others snuff out little lives before they have even seen the light of day, God who starts those lives takes note and will take account.

Every one of those little ones God sends into our families, into our world, is his miracle and intended to bring joy.

So special is each of them that God wants to put his name on every one. That's what Old Testament circumcision was, God's way of making that child his own, a member of his family, a sharer in the promise of the Savior given to Abraham. Today we use Holy Baptism to stamp the sign of the Savior's cross on the heart of our little ones. Through the washing of water with the Word, God works faith in them, wraps them in his Son's righteousness, writes their names in the Book of Life in heaven. "This child's name shall be Christian," we declare with grateful joy as we bring our little ones to that blessed baptismal font.

A very special prophet

No sooner had Zechariah finished writing "John" than he could speak. "He praised God," we are told. Surely praise was in order because of the special child God had given them. Yet the aged priest had more in mind. Nine months earlier in the temple, the angel had specifically announced what this child would become. "He will go on before the Lord," the angel had said, "to make ready a people prepared for the Lord" (Luke 1:17). Now with his speech returned and with the guidance of the Holy Spirit, Zechariah expands the thought, "You, my child, will be called a prophet of the Most High; for you will go on before the Lord to prepare the way for him, to give his people the knowledge of salvation through the forgiveness of their sins" (Luke 1:76,77).

What a special task God had in mind for their son. He was to be a very special prophet. Other prophets had to point across the centuries to the promised Savior. John could point across the waters of the Jordan in person to the Savior. Others predicted the coming of God's kingdom. John could announce, "The kingdom of heaven is at hand." Not only would John find joy in the Savior for himself; he would have that joy intensified by pointing many others to the Savior.

"What will our baby be?" parents wonder. Dream on, parents, dream of computer scientists and space engineers. Dream of artists and athletes. Dream of whatever. It makes no matter what your children become as long as they learn their purpose in life. God gives life to learn of the Savior and then to help others learn of him too. All children of God, wherever God places them, are called to be prophets, that is, to proclaim the glad tidings of the Savior to whomever, whenever they can.

As you wonder, though, parents, please remember John the Baptist. What nobler calling can there be for our children than to share with John the privilege of using their lives full-time to point others to the Lamb of God? The harvest still is plentiful, the workers still few, and the joy from working in the harvest fields is still out of this world.

Prayer: Thank you, Lord, for the gift of children. Lead parents everywhere to bring those little ones to your Son so that he may bless them. Lead them also to consider giving their children for full-time service in your harvest fields that many more may behold the Lamb of God. Amen.

"Whoever acknowledges me before men, I will also acknowledge him before my Father in heaven." (Matthew 10:32)

"Stand Up, Stand Up for Jesus"

It was June 25, 1530, not quite 13 years since a monk named Martin Luther had nailed up the Ninety-five Theses on the doors of the Castle Church in Wittenberg to start the Reformation. Much had happened in that short span. The truths of God's Word had spread across Germany in spite of the Roman Catholic Church's attacks on Luther. Through the restored message of the gospel, the Spirit had brought many to faith, including princes and leaders. Under Luther's guidance these hearty confessors of God's Word took their stand against opposing leaders of both church and state.

In 1530 Emperor Charles V, attempting to settle the religious controversy in his realm and to present a united front against the advancing Turkish horde, had once again called the leaders of church and state together, this time at Augsburg. The Lutherans were ready, not to give away any of the truth but to stand up for it. They had even prepared a document that both presented and defended their faith. And on June 25 it was read to the assembly gathered at Augsburg. What a document it was! Boldly, positively, clearly it set forth the truths of God's Word, not compromising with tepid language, but calling a spade a spade.

That document is called the Augsburg Confession. We still use it today in our church as a correct exposition of what Scripture teaches. Please ask your pastor for a copy and read it. You'll be glad you did. Rather than summarize that document here, let's take a look at our generation and consider what's involved in standing up for Jesus today, as those Lutherans did at Augsburg.

The problem

Of course, it's a problem to stand up for Jesus. It was for the disciples of Jesus' day. It was for Luther and the Christians of his day. And it's no less a problem today. If standing up for Jesus and his Word seems not too hazardous today, might it be not because the world has grown soft toward Christians, but Christians have grown soft toward the world? "Acknowledge," Jesus said, "say the same thing, identify with, take a stand with." "Me," he went on, "Jesus, with all that is involved in my person, my work, my teaching." "Before men," he added, "not in private where no one can see you, but openly, publicly, where others can see, examine, and benefit." In our church buildings we do it, in the safety of the sanctuary, surrounded by others of like mind and heart, repeating those words: "I believe in God, the Father almighty . . . [and] in Jesus Christ, his only Son, our Lord. . . . I believe in the Holy Spirit." But in the outside world, where life is lived, how goes it?

Christian teenager, what would you tell us? When the morals of the day, conditioned by the modern media, toss overboard whatever was once holy and sacred between man and woman, is it easy to stand up for Jesus? When the generation you belong to, labeled by the experts as the "post-Christian generation," tells you that truth is relative, that what you feel is right, how are you going to stand up for Jesus and his Word or even want to?

Christian adult, what would you tell us? Would it be of the difficulty in speaking up for Jesus in the family or neighborhood, in the market or workplace, because of the reception you receive when you try? Would it be with an apology for not trying too often because it's much easier, if not safer, to seal your lips and shut up your heart than to identify with Jesus and tell others about him?

Conservative church member, how about you? "Narrow-minded," the world calls us when we stand for unchanging truth and warn against error instead of reshaping or ignoring what the Word says. "Old-fashioned," they categorize us when we refuse to treat the Word like some Silly Putty to be molded into what "sells" today in the religious market. "A vanishing breed," they predict of us as they seem to leave us behind in the dust.

No, it's not easy to stand up for Jesus, as he asked of his disciples in their day and of our Lutheran forefathers in their day at Augsburg. But that's what our beloved Jesus requires of us and for good reason.

The promise

For those who stand up for him, Jesus has some beautiful words. He promises, "I will also acknowledge him before my Father in heaven." "I will acknowledge," Jesus said, "I, the Savior, I myself will stand beside such a one and claim him as my very own. Before my Father in heaven," he continued, "not just here on earth where nothing is permanent and everything passes away, but before my Father when the Last Day comes, in a heaven that is not only glorious but eternal."

We can almost imagine that scene in heaven when Jesus points to us: "Father, these people belong to me. I have paid for them with my own blood and have placed around them my robe of righteousness. By the work of the Spirit they know and trust in me as their only Savior. By the work of the Spirit they have shown their faith standing up for me on earth, even enduring the sneers and jeers of many. As you love me, so love them and let them stand around my throne through all eternity."

What generous words and what a glorious scene, especially because Jesus' confession of us in heaven will be pure grace. We won't deserve it nor can we earn it any more than we deserve or can earn our salvation. The faith in our hearts and the confession in our lives that Jesus finds will have been his gracious gifts to us, worked by his Spirit through Word and sacrament.

Until that day comes, there is only one way to stand up—stand up for Jesus. That's to stand in his strength alone! God help us. Amen.

Prayer: Stand up, stand up for Jesus! The strife will not be long;
This day the noise of battle, the next, the victor's song.
To him that overcometh a crown of life shall be;
He with the King of glory shall reign eternally. Amen.
(CW 474:4)

And he brought him [Simon] to Jesus.

Jesus looked at him and said, "You are Simon son of John. You will be called Cephas" (which, when translated, is Peter). (John 1:42)

Peter, the Disciple Who Was Much like Us

He talked when he should have been thinking. He slept when he should have been watching. He denied his Lord even after boasting that he never would. He misunderstood his master's mission even after having seen his glory. How much like us Peter was in his weakness. Yet look at what the Lord did with him just as the Savior also can do for us.

There's hope for us

What do you think Simon might tell us if we could meet him face-to-face? Might he have something to say about knowing our weaknesses? Knowing our strengths can lead to great accomplishments, but knowing our weaknesses can prevent even greater tragedy. If only Peter had recognized his pride! What sins and tears he might have avoided.

What is your weakness? Is it that same devilish pride that thinks we are so much and others so little and that shows in the way we treat them? Is it the sin of gossip that just can't rest until something tainted is heard or repeated about someone else? Is it alcohol or other things for which we reach to blot out problems and cure woes only to increase the pain? Is it gold and fingers that covet till we can never have enough? "Know your weakness," Peter might tell us, "the devil does, and if you don't, he'll win."

"Shed your tears," he might also tell us. Tears moisten our eyes when we watch a touching scene on TV or read one in a book, but how often do we shed tears over our sins? Our modern world weeps too little over sin, and we so often follow suit. When's the last time our sins really hit us? The last time we really stopped to think about the damnable difference between what God in his mercy wants us to be and what we actually are in daily life? That Maundy Thursday evening after he had so flagrantly denied his Lord, Peter finally knew, and his tears flowed. What about us?

But above all, Peter might say, "There's hope for you too." "Consistently inconsistent," Peter has been labeled. Doesn't that label also fit us? One moment in our need or grief we are deeply religious; the next, God seems a million miles away. One moment our faith seems so strong; the next, it's shot full of holes by doubts and questions. One moment we sincerely repent of our sins and earnestly intend with the aid of God the Holy Spirit to amend our sinful lives; the next, we are just as mean and irritable, uncharitable and unforgiving as before. "Consistently inconsistent"—yes, that describes us too. But Peter would tell us, "There's hope for you. Look at what the master did to me and what he wants to do to you."

There's strength for us

It took months of pounding and hammering, molding and shaping, but look what Jesus did to Simon. When Peter's faith and knowledge needed broadening, the master patiently taught him and repeated the lessons. When the boaster denied the Savior, Jesus looked on him and brought him to tears of repentance. When Easter Sunday came, the risen Lord came to him individually to stop his tears. And in the next few weeks the Lord restored him publicly to his discipleship, telling him, "Feed my lambs. . . . Feed my sheep" (John 21:15,17). As the Lord worked on him, more and more he became Peter the rock (which is the meaning of Cephas and Peter) and less and less clay was left in him. More and more he who had been so "consistently inconsistent" became "consistently strong."

Read the first 12 chapters of Acts and notice how Peter's strength shows. It was he who preached the sermon on Pentecost. It was he who, along with John, faced the hostile Sanhedrin and said, "We cannot help speaking about what we have seen and heard" (Acts 4:20). It was he who, when jailed for the second time, rejoiced that he was counted worthy to suffer shame for Jesus' name. Peter preached sermons, put up with imprisonment, prepared the way for work among the Gentiles, and if tradition is accurate, even died a martyr, crucified upside down, rather than deny his Lord—all with the strength Christ gave him.

What do you think Peter might tell us if we could meet with him? Might he say, "There's no use in even trying. You'll never become as strong as I"? Sometimes we might feel that way as we at best fumble and bumble our way along in trying to live our faith. Looking at Peter and then at ourselves, we might feel even more deeply how often we fail and how lukewarm and slow we are in our discipleship walk. "Don't even try." Do you think that's what Peter the rock would say to us?

Or would it be, "There's strength for you and you can find it in the same place I did"? It was Peter who wrote, "Like newborn babies, crave pure spiritual milk, so that by it you may grow up in your salvation" (1 Peter 2:2). And it was Peter who in his last recorded verse in Scripture urged: "Grow in the grace and knowledge of our Lord and Savior Jesus Christ. To him be glory both now and forever" (2 Peter 3:18).

Do we want to have more strength? To be more rock and less clay? Peter shows us how—through the Savior and his Word.

Prayer: Thank you, Lord Jesus, for not casting us aside when we so often have turned away from you, but instead looking for us as you once did for Simon Peter. Strengthen us, as you did Peter, removing the clay and adding the rock to our faith. Keep us in your Word through which you strengthen our faith and our resolve to live for you until the day when we stand perfectly strong and dedicated in heaven at your side. In your name we ask it. Amen.

I consider them rubbish, that I may gain Christ and be found in him, not having a righteousness of my own that comes from the law, but that which is through faith in Christ—the righteousness that comes from God and is by faith. I want to know Christ and the power of his resurrection. (Philippians 3:8-10)

"I Want to Know Christ"

Which words of the apostle Paul come to mind most frequently? Are they "I am not ashamed of the gospel, because it is the power of God for the salvation of everyone who believes" (Romans 1:16)? Or "I can do anything through him [Christ] who gives me strength" (Philippians 4:13)? Or "I resolved to know nothing while I was with you except Jesus Christ and him crucified" (1 Corinthians 2:2)?

When I think of the great apostle, one sentence in particular comes to mind, "I want to know Christ." That was Paul's burning desire, to know Christ more and more. That was also Paul's burning drive, to bring Christ to more and more.

Impossible

"I want to know Christ," Paul wrote. He didn't always talk that way. Once upon a time it was "I hate Christ and I want to destroy his followers." Why? Because Christ was a threat to Paul's way to heaven. When Jesus came along telling people like Saul the Pharisee that their thoughts about earning heaven through their own works were all wet, the defiant reaction was not "I want to know Jesus," but "I hate him and those who follow him." Nor could Saul do anything about it. Later he told the Ephesians, describing also his former spiritual condition, "You were dead in trespasses and sins." One sure future awaited Saul, and he had no more power than a dead man to change it.

And you and I? Of course we know Christ. Many of us can hardly remember a time when we didn't. But it wasn't always that way. Except for the grace of God, we'd still be trying to use the teaspoon of our own works to scratch out an impossible road to heaven. Like that lawyer sitting next to me on one flight to Mexico City. He was going to Acapulco, as he said with a smile, for rest and recreation; I was going to the barrios inland to visit our missionaries and their people. When I tried to witness to him about the Christ I knew, his reply was frosty: "I don't want to hear about your Christ. All I need is to be good, do good, and God will be good to me." How easily I could still have been like him. Left to myself, I'd still be like that pre-Damascus road Saul, finding it impossible to know Christ.

Incredible

Now listen to Paul in our reading. "Rubbish," he calls his former works and strivings, a word that actually means "manure," something we consider totally worthless and want out of our sight. Instead he shouts, "I want to gain Christ and be found in him, not having a righteousness of my own that comes from the law, but that which is through faith in Christ." Ever since that day on the Damascus road when the risen Christ had come to him, cracked open his dead heart, and changed his rebellious spirit, Paul had one treasure, one goal—to have Christ and to get to know him even better.

And you and I? Of course we say that we know Christ. But what do we mean? Is it like when someone asks, "Do you know so-and-so?" and we answer, "Yes, I met him the other day." Or is it like when we speak of our spouse: "I know her. We have lived and loved together for so-and-so many years. And yet I learn more about her every week." Need we ask which "know" Paul had in mind? He means to know Christ not as one who lived back in the centuries or up in the clouds of heaven, but as the one who loves me and gave himself for me. He means to know that because of Christ's death my Father has hit the delete key and totally erased my debt in his heavenly computer. He means to know that in Christ I have victory spelled L-I-F-E when death comes stalking me. And he means that I keep growing in my knowledge of Christ by going regularly into his Word.

Unstoppable

If there is one word we might use to describe Paul after his conversion, it would have to be *unstoppable*. From that Damascus road where he first saw Christ, he went out to the known roads of his world to tell others about Christ. He crisscrossed the world of his time on three extensive missionary journeys. He even planned and perhaps got to Spain, the outpost of his world. He just had to tell others. "I am obligated," he told the Romans, "both to Greeks and non-Greeks, both to the wise and the foolish. That is why I am so eager to preach the gospel also to you who are at Rome" (Romans 1:14).

And you and I? It's not enough to say, "I know Christ." Not enough to say, "My spouse knows him." Not even enough to say, "My kids and grandkids know him." To know Christ is to want others to know him too. So whom have I told lately? How about my neighbors, not just those of the same color and culture but also those who are different? How about my relatives, even though that's not always the easiest? How about those nameless, faceless people in those cities with mushrooming populations and in those countries with names we can hardly pronounce? What about that synod side of our offering envelopes or synodical percentage of our congregational offering? We can model Christ with our daily lives, tell of Christ when the opportunity presents itself, pray for those who go to tell others in our place, and support them with our gifts of love. All this with one purpose in mind, that others might also know Christ and have in him the joy you and I share.

"I want to know Christ." By God's incredible grace, the impossible has happened to you and me. Now let our efforts to tell others be unstoppable too.

Prayer: I hear the Savior calling! His call has urgency!
Each moment souls are dying; soon comes eternity.
And so, my precious Savior, this is my humble plea:
Prepare me for my mission for you are calling me! Amen.
(CW 560:5)

St. Mary Magdalene (July 22)

Early on the first day of the week, while it was still dark, Mary Magdalene went to the tomb and saw that the stone had been removed from the entrance. So she came running to Simon Peter and the other disciple, the one Jesus loved, and said, "They have taken the Lord out of the tomb, and we don't know where they have put him!" (John 20:1,2)

Can You See the Light?

The road, on one of my trips for our Board for World Missions, took me through the mountains of Norway. The first tunnel we entered was over three kilometers long. What a feeling, almost scary, to leave the bright sun behind and enter that dimly lit, seemingly endless tunnel. How our eyes almost longed for the first glimmer of light as we neared the exit. And how our spirits lifted as we drove out again into the beautiful, warm sunshine.

Mary Magdalene knew something about what we were feeling that day, only in much greater depth. That first Easter Sunday she was one of the first ones to see the light at the end of the tunnel.

Darkness

Mary came to Jesus' tomb early. "While it was still dark," John writes. And those words just about describe the condition of her heart too. Anyone who has lost a loved one knows something about how she must have felt—the loss, the despair, the grief over one who is gone, never to return again.

But Mary's darkness went much deeper. Remember her past months. She had been cured by Jesus when he had cast seven devils out of her. From then on she had followed him, serving him with full devotion and a heart full of faith in him as the promised Savior. Then had come Good Friday. Not only was the sky over Calvary pitch black as she stood beneath Christ's cross, so was her heart. Not only was the tomb into which they hurriedly deposited his lifeless clay devoid of light, so was her spirit. Not only was Jesus dead, so were her hopes that he was the one who would redeem Israel. Now even his body was gone, the last remnant she had of him, carried off by who knows whom to who knows where. Yes, "while it was dark" described not only the sky but also her soul.

Is there anyone reading this who knows the feeling? Anyone who's wept at a freshly filled grave or who's returned to weep again and again? Anyone who's struggling with life, getting tired of its burdens and weary of its weight? Anyone whose sins just never seem to go away and whose temptations so often seem to win? Anyone who's feeling shoved into some tunnel without any daylight in sight? Then stick around as we follow Mary Magdalene from darkness into dawn.

Dawn

Dawn comes. Every day it happens. So also that first Easter. In the early glimmer of light that day, Mary could see that the stone had been rolled away from Jesus' tomb. Just a little thinking and Mary should have known the disciples had not cracked open the master's tomb and stolen his body to spread the lie that he was risen from the dead. They were too paralyzed by fear to plan and perform such things. A little more thinking and she should have known that the enemies had nothing to do with the rolled-away stone either. In fact, that was the very thing they were trying to prevent with their round-the-clock guard and special seal. They wanted Jesus still dead in that tomb so people could start forgetting all about him and settle back to normal again. But the Easter dawn was starting. Some of her friends had continued on to the tomb, even though she had turned back. And they had not only seen angels shining in glory but heard the unbelievable news that Jesus was risen from the dead.

Is there anyone reading this who knows the feeling? Anyone who's ever walked away from the worship service feeling good only to have life as usual dim the joy? Anyone who's seen the Easter dawning only to have pain and problem, loss and doubt like some dropping curtain shut out almost all the Easter light? Then stick around as we follow Mary Magdalene from dawn into full daylight.

Daylight

Dawn soon disappears, chased away by the sun rising in all its glory. In the dawn Mary had seen the stone rolled away and had run back to Jerusalem to report, "They have taken the Lord out of the tomb and we don't know where they have put him." Later in the daylight she returned to that tomb to weep and tell the angel the same story.

Then it happened. As she wept, she turned and through tear-blurred eyes noticed someone standing behind her. All doubt vanished as she heard that voice she knew so well calling out, "Mary." With amazing suddenness her tears were dried and the weight lifted from her heart. No more could sin's guilt hammer her; Christ had been delivered for her sins and raised again for her justification. No more could Satan bedevil her; Christ had marched into his hellish domain and dropped him flat in the dust. No more could death hold her; Christ had both entered and exited the grave to show that because he lives so would she. The tunnel of darkness was left far behind as she thrilled to the news, "My Savior lives."

Is there anyone reading this who knows the feeling? I hope so. The glorious light of Easter brightens our darkest day and keeps the smile of faith on our lips. Long after our graves are forgotten and the etching faded on our gravestones, this Easter light will still be shining. As long as the world stands, people like Mary Magdalene will find their greatest joy in him who is the resurrection and the life.

Prayer: Risen Lord, thank you for the glorious light of Easter. Help us live each day in its light. When the sins and troubles of life threaten to plunge us into darkness, help us see you standing at the end of the tunnel. Keep our faith strong till in heaven we see you face-to-face, as Mary Magdalene did that first Easter. Amen.

It was about this time that King Herod arrested some who belonged to the church, intending to persecute them. He had James, the brother of John, put to death with the sword. (Acts 12:1,2)

James the Elder, the Disciple Who Shows Us the Formula for Strength

Take a flat round of dough, add some tomato sauce, sprinkle with cheese and sausage, and what do you get? Everyone, or almost everyone, would answer, "Pizza." That's the recipe, or formula, for pizza.

Ready for another formula? One that ought to concern each one of us? Take the believer who's still a sinner even after being brought to faith, add the Savior, and what do you get? "People like James the Elder" is the answer.

Take the sinner

James is one of the quiet disciples. In Scripture he's never mentioned by himself. Always it's "James and his brother John." Nor do we have any sentences that he spoke by himself. In the two sentences that might be attributed to him, the words are said to have come from both James and John. Humanly speaking, it would have been better if they had spoken neither of those two sentences.

The first sentence shows misguided anger. The scene was a dusty road somewhere in Samaria, sometime after Christ's transfiguration. It was time to bed down for the night. James and John had gone into the village near at hand to find lodging, only to be rebuffed. The Samaritans in that town wanted nothing to do with a group of Jews, their traditional enemies. "How could they reject the master?" those brothers fumed. They then erupted with an angry request to Jesus, "Lord, do you want us to call fire down from heaven to destroy them?" (Luke 9:51-55). That's when they received a rebuke from the master and the nickname "Boanerges," or "Sons of Thunder."

James and his brother John spoke the second sentence on the final journey to Jerusalem, with the countdown to the cross well under way (Mark 10:35-45). Again their sentence was a request, this time one of misguided ambition. Surely all this solemn talk about going to Jerusalem must have meant that Christ's kingdom was near. Those two brothers could only think in terms of an earthly kingdom and the right- and left-hand top spots for them in that kingdom. The Savior, whose one ambition was to serve in humble love, had to scold these believers for their sinful request.

Sound familiar? We're believers, disciples, like James the Elder. Our lives and our deaths revolve around that Jesus. Yet we are sinners whose knowledge is marred by ignorance and whose faith is laced with unbelief. Misguided anger and misguided ambition are no strangers to us either. "Why doesn't God let the bombs fall?" we fume when something happens in the world. "How come I don't get recognition for the work I do for the congregation?" we grumble inside. "Surely I'm not as bad, if not much better," we croon as we line ourselves up against others. Yes, it's true. We still are sinners like James the Elder.

Add the Savior

So what's the answer? Isn't that obvious? You add the Savior. That's the foolproof part of the formula. Look at James.

Jesus didn't just rebuke him for his misguided anger and leave him with ears burning with shame. Instead, he lovingly corrected him. "James," he said, "don't you know that the Son of Man is not come to destroy lives, but to save them?" The Son of Man came to go to the cross, to have hellfire fall on him so that sinners might be spared. In the cross is the answer when it's time to forgive others. In the cross also is the answer for misguided ambition. When James and John came jockeying for earthly position, Jesus reminded them, "The Son of Man did not come to be served, but to serve, and to give his life as a ransom for many." Greatness in the kingdom is not measured by lofty position, but loving service, as the master showed with his cross.

Aren't you glad that Jesus doesn't shut the book on us? That he doesn't scratch out our names in the Book of Life every time we sin? Instead, he comes to us again and again, scolding us when he must, but then reassuring us of his ever-ready forgiveness through his Holy Word and sacraments. Yes, thank God the formula reads, "Take the sinner and add the Savior."

And get strength

The result will be strength for us as it was for James. When King Herod Agrippa after Christ's ascension wanted to stem the surging tide of Christianity, he reached for James the Elder. Was this like lightning striking the tallest, most prominent object? Was it James' zeal for Christ that marked him for the sword as the first of the disciples to die? We aren't told, but this much we can safely say. When you take the sinner and add the Savior, the result is strength even to lay down one's life.

"I promise to suffer all, even death, rather than to fall away from him," was one of the answers we gave on our confirmation day. Did we realize what we were saying? Or did it appear not too serious, since we couldn't recall the last time we had heard of someone dying for Jesus? Perhaps we should turn that answer around and say, "I promise to suffer all, even life, rather than to fall away from him." It's hard enough living for Jesus, much less even thinking about dying for him. Much preferred is a sort of air-conditioned Christianity, rather than one that asks us to sweat for Jesus. Far more palatable is an easy kind of religious life where we set the conditions, rather than where Jesus, who gave his all for us, makes his demands on us.

Strange, though, how that all can change when we follow James' formula, where you take the sinner, add liberal doses of the Savior and his Word, and end up with strength, not only to die, but also to live for him.

Prayer: Thank you, Lord, for not discarding us because of our many sins, but instead taking hell's punishment for them. Help us realize that the closer we are to you the more we can fight against sin and work to serve you. Bless our use of your Holy Word and sacraments for the strengthening of our faith and zeal in your service. Amen.

St. Mary, Mother of Our Lord (August 15)

And Mary said:

> "My soul glorifies the Lord
>   and my spirit rejoices in God my Savior,
> for he has been mindful
>   of the humble state of his servant.
> From now on all generations will call me blessed,
>   for the Mighty One has done great things for me—
>   holy is his name." (Luke 1:46-49)

Sing Along with Mary

For several moments at the stoplight, I watched the person in the other car. She was singing along, her head swaying, her hands keeping beat with the tune on the car radio. In fact, she had it turned up so loudly that I could have joined in.

When's the last time we sang along with someone? Hopefully, we'd want to join Mary as she sings her joyful hymn.

Because of her Savior

Mary was in the house of her relative Elizabeth, having hurried there to share some good news. But before she could even begin, Elizabeth told her all about it, how Mary was blessed among women because of having been chosen to give birth to the promised Savior. What wonderful strengthening for Mary's faith this must have been, to have Elizabeth tell her the same news that the angel Gabriel had. Now Mary's heart overflowed with grateful faith and fervent joy. Because her heart was full, her lips sang.

"My soul glorifies the Lord," she sang. Mary was not concerned about praise for herself. There was no pride flooding her heart because of what she was going to do. Praise was in order, very much so, and it could go in only one direction, to the Lord. Miraculously pregnant with the Son of God, she could only marvel at the "Mighty One" who was doing "such great things" for her.

What were the "great things" the mighty God was doing for her? Mary points them out clearly. "My spirit rejoices in God my Savior," she sings. "God," she calls him, using a term that means the "God of might," the "all-powerful God." "Savior," she also calls him, identifying him as the one who used his great power to accomplish something that was great beyond measure, the salvation of sinners. But above all, she uses that little word, "my." That blessed baby in her womb was her Savior. She was singing with joy because her almighty God was giving her what she needed most—a Savior from her sins. As one church father wrote, "Mary was more blessed in that she believed in Christ, than in that she had given him birth."

Rose was her name. She had had an illustrious career, one that had taken her to many countries. But she was an unbeliever until in her early 80s. Barely two years after her adult baptism, she was struck down with a vicious, quick-spreading malignancy. At my last visit to her hospital bed, she asked me to close the door and then confessed some details of her past life. When she was all done, somehow the Spirit gave me the right words. "Rose," I said, "where sin increased, grace increased all the more" (Romans 5:20). Those were the last words I ever spoke to her. As I left that hospital room, I heard her repeating softly with joy, "Grace increased all the more." Sing along with Mary because of the gift of her Savior? Rose did!

And us? God has done so many great things for us. From the hearts that beat regularly inside our chests to the loved ones who stand faithfully at our sides, from the daily food on our tables to the daily opportunities in our lives, God does so much for us. Do we take such great gifts for granted? Of course, we have to admit rather shamefacedly. We even take his greatest gift of all for granted. "He's my Savior," we say too, but do we say it often enough? And when we do, is it with the same kind of zeal that Mary put forth in her song? Is it with that amazed awe, that mouth-wide-open kind of marveling at what a great thing it is God has done for us? We can never sing along with Mary too often because of God's greatest gift, our Savior.

Because of his favor

"Why?" Mary must have asked a number of times during the months of her pregnancy, "Why did God pick me to give birth to the Savior?" In her song she gives the answer. It was because a gracious God was "mindful of the humble state of his servant." Mary also was mindful of her "humble state," of how in God's eyes she was nothing but a sinner and deserved nothing from him but punishment. She knew her state, admitted it, and was thankful that in spite of it God had favored her with the great privilege of giving birth to the Savior of the world. So favored by a gracious God, Mary's heart flowed over with thankful song.

Just as amazing as God's choice of lowly Mary is his choice of us. We didn't choose him; he chose us. We didn't come seeking him; he came seeking us. It was not our worthiness; it was his favor. It's time to take out our baptismal certificates again and marvel anew at how God favored us with his grace. He put the sign of his Son's cross on our hearts, wrote our names in his Book of Life in heaven, solely because of his grace! It's time to pay special attention as in each sermon we hear how he gave his one and only Son, not just to be the Savior of the world but our Savior too, and of how solely because of his grace, he has changed that "*whoever* believes in him shall not perish" into our names. It's time to stand at that Communion altar to feel his hand on our shoulders and see his love-filled eyes looking at us, as he offers us his very body and blood in assurance of every sin forgiven in our lowly lives, solely because of his grace.

When we do, no one will have to tell us to sing along with Mary.

Prayer: Lord, what great things you have done for us, sending the Savior for undeserving sinners. Accept our songs of praise as we raise them to your glorious throne. Then help us translate those songs into lives that resound with praise for you daily. In the Savior's name we ask it. Amen.

St. Bartholomew, Apostle (August 24)

Philip found Nathanael and told him, "We have found the one Moses wrote about in the Law, and about whom the prophets also wrote—Jesus of Nazareth, the son of Joseph."

"Nazareth! Can anything good come from there?" Nathanael asked.

"Come and see," said Philip.

When Jesus saw Nathanael approaching, he said of him, "Here is a true Israelite, in whom there is nothing false."

"How do you know me?" Nathanael asked.

Jesus answered, "I saw you while you were still under the fig tree before Philip called you."

Then Nathanael declared, "Rabbi, you are the Son of God; you are the King of Israel."

Jesus said, "You believe because I told you I saw you under the fig tree. You shall see greater things than that." He then added, "I tell you the truth, you shall see heaven open, and the angels of God ascending and descending on the Son of Man." (John 1:45-51)

Bartholomew, the Disciple We'd Like to Imitate

Modeling is the way to go. If you want people to learn, don't just tell them; show them. Or as a wise man once said, "What you do speaks so loudly I can't hear what you say." It's the same with discipleship. Looking at Bartholomew, also known as Nathanael, we have an example we surely would like to imitate.

Searching the Scriptures

Nathanael searched the Scriptures. He knew what they had to say. When his friend Philip came all excited that day to tell him, "We have found the one Moses wrote about in the Law, and about whom the prophets wrote—Jesus of Nazareth, the son of Joseph," Nathanael wasn't so sure. He knew the Old Testament and how it pointed not to Nazareth, but to Bethlehem. So he had to ask, "Nazareth! Can anything good come from there?" Note also where Philip found him, under the wide-spreading branches of the fig tree, a secluded, shaded spot where he could well have been searching the Scriptures.

We need more fig trees! In our hurry, scurry world, where we are so geared to going that we don't even stop to ask where, we need to slow down and make time to search the Scriptures. They speak to us of Christ, the only way to heaven, a way we need to know as fully as possible. They speak to us about God's will and ways, something we surely want to know and follow. Such knowledge doesn't miraculously drop down from heaven or filter into our minds as we sleep. It comes from searching the Scriptures.

Showing nothing false

Philip didn't waste time arguing, but simply answered, "Come and see." And see Nathanael did. As he drew near, he heard Jesus say, "Here is a true Israelite, in whom there is nothing false." How did Jesus know him? The two of them had never met. Even more so, how did the master know that Nathanael was a sincere and honest Israelite who was no phony, but one eagerly waiting for the Savior to come? Jesus had the answer, "I saw you while you were still under the fig tree before Philip called you." There could be only one conclusion. With guileless faith, given him by the Spirit, Nathanael answered, "You are the Son of God; you are the King of Israel."

Every pastor worth his salt prays for many things for his members. Chief among them is the prayer, "Lord, give us more Nathanaels." Members who not only sing but show that Jesus is their "Beautiful Savior." Who not only sing but show by their use "How precious is the Book divine." Who not only sing, "Take my life and let it be, consecrated, Lord, to thee," but show they mean it. Who not only sing, "Here am I, send me, send me," but then go where he sends them. Needed are more Nathanaels, in whom there is nothing false.

Seeing greater things

"You shall see greater things," Jesus promised Nathanael. "You shall see heaven open, and the angels of God ascending and descending on the Son of Man." Did Nathanael later think of this promise when he saw the master healing the sick and raising the dead? when he heard Jesus speak of the rooms in the Father's house and of the one way there? when he saw the empty tomb and the risen Lord? What greater things could he ever see than this? Sin was paid for, death conquered, heaven opened. Jesus was the ladder linking earth and heaven, the one way for a sinner to climb to the Father's house above. And who could even faintly guess at the greater things awaiting the believer at the end of that ladder in heaven?

Do you see why we label Bartholomew as the disciple we'd like to imitate? He reminds us vividly that the greatest thing you and I can see in life is the Savior. There's nothing more important for us to know than the One who loves us and gave himself for us. Such knowledge at once handles life's greatest problem, our sins. There's nothing more important for us either than to know that Jesus goes with us always, even to the ends of the earth. Such knowledge at once handles the bumps and bruises, even the collisions and near-fatal mishaps in life. And surely there's nothing more important for us than, when our final moment comes, to know he will say, "Today you will be with me in paradise" (Luke 23:43). Such knowledge takes the sting out of death's certainty and the unknown out of its finality. With Nathanael we can see no greater thing than Jesus, our Savior and King, the Lord of our life and our death.

Call him Nathanael or call him Bartholomew, it doesn't matter. What does matter is that our gracious Lord will help us imitate him.

Prayer: Lord, give us such a faith as this,
And then, whatever may come,
We'll taste even now the hallowed bliss
Of an eternal home. Amen. (CW 405:6)

St. Matthew, Apostle   (September 21)

As Jesus went on from there, he saw a man named Matthew sitting at the tax collector's booth. "Follow me," he told him, and Matthew got up and followed him.

While Jesus was having dinner at Matthew's house, many tax collectors and "sinners" came and ate with him and his disciples. (Matthew 9:9,10)

Matthew, the Disciple Who Was Qualified by Grace

Ice cream never tasted so good! Back in the late 1930s, one of the highlights of the week was the pint of ice cream my father bought after church on Sunday. It was divided among the six of us, and every one of the few spoonfuls we received was a treat. Now we have it in bulk in the home freezer and no longer treasure it so highly.

Is that how we at times view our discipleship? Something we've had for so long and in such measure that we take it for granted? If so, perhaps there's a lesson for us in Matthew's call to discipleship, one that reminds us so vividly of God's grace.

What we might have remained

What might Matthew have remained if God's grace had not called him that day? Among other things, perhaps a rather disliked and distrusted tax collector. Taxes have never been popular, and when the tax collection system was riddled with corruption, as Rome's was, we can understand how the dislike grew. A Jew turned tax collector lost his standing among his fellow citizens. They would no longer allow him to worship in the synagogue or accept his word in court. He was classed with the scum of society.

Such was Matthew at whose desk Jesus stopped. To the outward eye, even if Matthew were one of those rare ones who kept his skirts clean, his credentials for discipleship were skimpy indeed. To Jesus' eye there were no credentials at all. When the master looked at Matthew, he saw the same things once visible in us. He saw unbelief and sin. That's what Matthew was and would have remained—but for the grace of God!

They tell us that less than 25 percent of the world's current five billion people can be called Christian. That means that three out of every four people alive right now either haven't heard of Jesus or, having heard, don't have Jesus. They also tell us that at the present population growth rate, by the time a baby born today graduates from high school, another two billion will have been added to the world's population. And most of them will have been born among people who are, for the most part, non-Christian.

What do such statistics shout out at us? Do we realize what our chances were of remaining in the ranks of unbelievers? Do we realize what the chances were of our children and grandchildren never leaving those ranks in a burgeoning world? From Matthew comes the vivid reminder of what we too might have remained—but for the grace of God!

What we instead became

"Follow me," Jesus said, and Matthew did. Called and moved by grace, he walked in the company of the master. For Matthew discipleship meant getting. Great were the things he received, all that the Savior had to offer. Tax careers and custom receipts must have seemed petty compared to the treasures received from Christ.

For Matthew, discipleship also meant giving. One form his giving took was the holding of a dinner party for Jesus. In the parallel account (Luke 5:29), it appears that he gave this party just as much for his friends as for Jesus. Was Matthew hoping that by talking and listening to Jesus, his friends would find what he had received? So the tax collector became a soul gatherer, the recipient, a sharer—by the grace of God! Matthew still shares today. His legacy to all of us is the inspired gospel that bears his name. In it he gives convincing testimony of what treasures await us in Christ Jesus.

Would we want to give up what God's grace has given us? Such a thought horrifies us. No beautiful Savior to tell me, "My blood purifies you from every sin." No heavenly Friend to remind me, "Never will I leave you; never will I forsake you." No mighty Victor to calm me, "Because I live, you also will live." No loving Judge to welcome me, "Come, take your inheritance, the kingdom prepared for you." Who would ever want to lose such treasures?

Still the nagging question remains, "How come I'm not more eager to share such treasures with others?" How concerned am I about that three-fourths of the world's population that doesn't profess Christianity? How concerned am I about the world mission thrust I help carry on through my synod? Does it bother me to hear that my synod has expatriate missionaries working in barely two handfuls of countries besides my own? Does it bother me to hear that less than four cents out of every dollar given by the members of my synod for overall church work goes to world missions?

Does such information only momentarily alarm and mildly disturb us? Or does it make us more eager to share what God's grace has given us and even to sweat in trying?

Prayer: Lord, when we look at the rich forgiveness you have prepared for us and the faith to receive what you have given us, we have to thank you for your grace. Help us appreciate the gift of your grace and then help us show that appreciation in our desire to share your grace with a needy world, as Matthew did. Let your Word and the spreading of it occupy our hearts, receive our daily efforts, and call forth our honest offerings that more may praise you for your grace. Amen.

St. Michael and All Angels (September 29)

The seventy-two returned with joy and said, "Lord, even the demons submit to us in your name."

He replied, "I saw Satan fall like lightning from heaven. I have given you authority to trample on snakes and scorpions and to overcome all the power of the enemy; nothing will harm you. However, do not rejoice that the spirits submit to you, but rejoice that your names are written in heaven." (Luke 10:17-20)

Why Do the Angels Smile?

"Why are the angels smiling?" asked the kindergartner. One of the children, as I was explaining the various items in the church, had his eyes fixed on the sculpted angels that decorated the points where the soaring arches met their supporting columns. He wasn't listening to me, but was looking at the smile on the face of each angel.

Of course the angels smile. They are present when God's people worship (1 Corinthians 11:10), find joy when the news of God's salvation is proclaimed (Luke 2:10,11), and rejoice greatly when sinners are brought to repentance (Luke 15:10). And we want to smile with them for the same reasons.

The disciples had a good answer

Pair by pair the 72 returned from their mission, bubbling over with joy. Excitedly they reported their success, capping it off with, "Lord, even the demons submit to us in your name." Using Jesus' power they had been able to subdue demons, those angels once created holy by God, but then fallen into sin, and now sent by Satan, their hellish captain, to bedevil people on earth.

The 72 in their joy were telling Jesus nothing new. Their master had gone with them in spirit and seen their success over the powers of darkness. He had seen Satan, like some jagged bolt of lightning, sent hurtling from his seat of power to the ground. Just as promised in the Garden of Eden, Christ had begun the crushing of Satan's head and would finish the job on Calvary's cross. It was no accident that the disciples could subdue demons. Behind their victories stood Christ's upcoming victory over Satan. Because of that victory, the disciples would be able to "overcome all the power of the enemy." With these words Jesus was not promising them supernatural ability to walk over snakes and scorpions but heavenly mastery over Satan and his evil angels. Regardless of how the forces from hell would connive to inject their poison into human veins, the disciples would have the antidote in God's Word.

Every time we hold a home devotion, bring our families to church, apply the gospel to our loved ones or our neighbors, we are causing Satan to topple. Every time we support Christ's church with our efforts, prayers, offerings, we are following in the footsteps of the 72. With Jesus' power as it works through the Word, we can foster kingdom growth in our house and yours, in our hometowns and across the world, in Hong Kong and Honolulu. If it were possible for us to see this growth and report back to our Lord as those disciples did, wouldn't it be with smiles on our faces and joy in our voices? And the angels would smile with us.

Jesus had an even better answer

What we can do for Christ with his gospel causes us to rejoice. Even greater joy can be found, though, in what

Christ has done for us. Jesus told the 72, "Rejoice that your names are written in heaven." Not what we can do for Jesus, but what Jesus has done for us is our best reason for smiling.

What has Jesus done for us? He sums it up with a most delightful picture used several times in both the Old and New Testaments. It's as if God keeps a family record in heaven, something like our forefathers used to have in their family Bibles, where all the names of the children and grandchildren were recorded. The omniscient Lord needs no written record, for he knows all his children intimately, with their names written permanently in his loving memory. He lists us as his redeemed, restored, forgiven children and heirs of his heaven. That's more than cause for rejoicing.

How did our names come to be written in the Book of Heaven? Obviously, we had nothing to do with it. If we had our own way and say, our names would still be on Satan's register with an eternal room number in hell assigned to us. But God in his inscrutable grace and indescribable love recorded our names in heaven. Into this world and onto a cross he sent the most precious thing he had, his own Son. In this world his Son took on our flesh and our sins, even to the point of submitting to the inhuman tortures of crucifixion and the full force of hell's fury for every sin. Even more, into our stony hearts he then sent and keeps sending his Holy Spirit to call us by the gospel, enlighten us with his gifts, sanctify us, and keep us in the true faith. This in brief is what it cost the triune God to have a sinner's name recorded in heaven. If our names are recorded there by God's golden pen dipped in Christ's crimson blood, should that not be our greatest reason for smiling with joy?

Why do the angels smile? For the same reason we do when we see the gospel doing its work and sinners being called to repentance. Come to think of it, don't we have reason to smile even more broadly than those holy angels? After all, we are the sinners who are called to repentance and whose names are written in heaven.

Prayer: Father, how do we thank you for the overwhelming joy that comes from being your children? For your rich love in sending Jesus to be the Savior and for your unmerited grace in sending your Spirit to work faith in our hearts, we thank you. Hold before our eyes always the wondrous truth that by your grace our names are written in heaven, till in heaven we behold in full what that joyful promise means. In the Savior's name we ask it. Amen.

Many have undertaken to draw up an account of the things that have been fulfilled among us, just as they were handed down to us by those who from the first were eyewitnesses and servants of the word. Therefore, since I myself have carefully investigated everything from the beginning, it seemed good also to me to write an orderly account for you, most excellent Theophilus, so that you may know the certainty of the things you have been taught. (Luke 1:1-4)

"I Love to Tell the Story of Jesus and His Love"

When's the last time you've read the first four verses of Luke's gospel? Some sections in Scripture we almost skip over because they don't seem to say much to us, like the first half of chapter 1 of Matthew's gospel. There we find name after name, some of them hard to pronounce, listed in a genealogy that appears to have little meaning for us. But when we stop to read more carefully, we discover those names show that Jesus is the promised Messiah, who indeed did come from the house of David, the tribe of Judah, and is the seed of Abraham, just as God had promised.

When we stop to reread the first four verses of Luke's gospel, we also find much. From these personal words with which Luke begins his gospel, we gain a sense of what Jesus meant to him and how much Luke wanted to share him with others. This gospel was written by . . .

One who loved Jesus

Who was this Luke mentioned by name only three times in the Bible, all of them in Paul's epistles? His name means "belonging to the light," though we don't know how he came to know the one and only light, Jesus Christ. By birth he was a Gentile and by profession, a doctor, perhaps even the apostle Paul's personal physician (Colossians 4:10-14). More so, he was Paul's valued companion and valuable coworker (2 Timothy 4:11; Philemon 24). With Paul on both the second and third missionary journeys, Luke also remained at the apostle's side during the imprisonments and right up to the end in Rome. Sounds like the kind of loyal, capable person we would want at our sides.

Above all, Luke was one who loved Jesus. How do we know? He wanted to share all that he could about the Savior with an acquaintance whom he calls "most excellent Theophilus." And for the best reason of all, that Theophilus, probably a high Roman official, might "know the certainty of the things you have been taught." Was this man in Luke's adult instruction class? How much had he already been taught? How much did he already believe? We aren't told, but what we do know is that Luke wanted to tell him more of the story, the only story that counted, of Jesus and his love. What Luke the evangelist, inspired by the Holy Spirit, wrote for Theophilus has been preserved by the same Spirit for us today.

My father loved animals, raising them, working with them, even as part of his livelihood hauling them to the stockyards and the county fairs. From little on he took me along, with my short legs dangling off the truck seat or hustling to keep up with him in the horse barns at the fair. Again and again he would point to an animal and say to me, "Do you see that? That's what you look for in a cow." Or "That's what makes a horse good." What he loved he wanted others to love. What he knew he wanted others to know also. He did the same thing to me with Jesus!

What will people say about us someday? Will it be, he or she knew how to run a computer and do spreadsheets? how to be a police officer or an administrator? how to manage a family? It could be, depending on what the Lord gives us and where he puts us. But even more so, wouldn't we want people to say, he or she knew Jesus and wanted others to know him too? or he or she loved to tell the story wherever and in whatever way God indicated?

One who loved all

Luke wrote not only for Theophilus but for the world. Reading his gospel, we quickly catch his concern for presenting Jesus as the Savior who came for all, rich and poor, high official and outcast sinner, Jew and Gentile, man, woman, and child. He wrote to present a Savior of whom everyone could claim, "He is my Savior."

It's in Luke's gospel that we find the parables of the lost sheep, lost coin, and lost son, illustrating Jesus' concern for the recovery of the straying. It's in his gospel too where we find the woman with the shadowy past whose tears washed Jesus' feet because of his tender mercy for her. From Luke's account of Jesus' loving, forgiving dealings with tax collector Zacchaeus comes the sweet, succinct summary of Jesus' mission, "The Son of Man came to seek and to save what was lost." Jesus' tears over stubborn Jerusalem, his prayer for those who crucified him, his promise for the thief hanging next to him are found where else but in the gospel of Luke. Throughout his book plays the sweet refrain of Jesus' love for all kinds of people in all kinds of needs. Is it any wonder that the Holy Spirit also used Doctor Luke to write the book of Acts, in which we find detailed how the story of this Savior of all was carried out into all the world?

Luke's work is not complete till you and I know and love this Savior. Praise God he moved Luke to tell us about the friend of sinners and the redeemer of the lost. Thank God he sends his Spirit to work through what Luke has written so that we also can say, "He is my Savior." Pray to God that he would fill us with the same zeal to tell others the story of Jesus and his love.

Prayer: Thank you, Lord, for telling us the story of Jesus and his love. Please help us love to tell it to others, till in heaven it is our theme in glory. Amen.

St. James of Jerusalem

James, a servant of God and of the Lord Jesus Christ,

To the twelve tribes scattered among the nations:

Greetings.

Consider it pure joy, my brothers, whenever you face trials of many kinds, because you know that the testing of your faith develops perseverance. Perseverance must finish its work so that you may be mature and complete, not lacking anything. (James 1:1-4)

James, a Practical Man with a Practical Message

Among the four men named James in the New Testament was one we call James of Jerusalem. He was not one of the Twelve chosen by Jesus. Instead, he was among those identified as the master's brothers and sisters, very likely later children of Mary and Joseph. Though part of Jesus' family, he apparently did not accept his brother as the promised Messiah until the risen Lord appeared personally to him (1 Corinthians 15:7).

From that time on, James of Jerusalem stands out as a pillar in the early church, having great influence among Jewish believers. It was James with whom Paul consulted upon coming to Jerusalem after his conversion (Galatians 1:18,19). It was James who at the first church convention in Jerusalem stood up and gave practical advice as to how to integrate gentile believers into what had been up to that point basically a Jewish church (Acts 15:13-21). Most scholars also believe it was this James who under the inspiration of the Holy Spirit penned the epistle bearing his name.

A practical man

Notice what James calls himself. "A servant [actually, slave] of God and of the Lord Jesus Christ," he identifies himself to his readers, the Jewish Christians scattered throughout the Roman world of the first century. There's no reference to position or prominence, only to that which really matters, his relationship to his Lord and Savior. Here was a man whose heart and will were humbly obedient and whose life and all were completely committed to Jesus Christ, his God and Lord. Here was a Christian whose heart trusted in Jesus and whose life showed that he did.

Notice also how quickly James gets down to brass tacks. Without skipping a beat, he plunges ahead with practical advice as to how the Christian is to view adversity. If we were to flip ahead in his epistle, we would find the same practicality, so much so that some have labeled his book the "Epistle of Practicality." From beginning to end, it presents an urgent demand for reality in religion. His words are painfully practical, urging his readers to match profession with performance and creed with conduct. Repeatedly he reminds his readers that "high talk and low walk" are out of place among Christians.

We dare not misunderstand James. He's not promoting Christian living as a means of earning heaven. That Jesus Christ has done once for all. What James is saying is that those who are filled with and fueled by Christ's great love will live like Christians. Though James seldom mentions the Savior by name in his letter, we soon see his bright light shining on every page and his love moving behind every practical admonition.

Think we can benefit by listening to such a practical man? Each generation likes to think that the questions it asks and the problems it faces are new. Listening to James will show again that though problems may vary in shape and size, little more than the calendar separates the Christian of today from the one of James' day.

A practical message

For example, listen to what James has to say about facing trials. When trials come, James urges his readers, don't resent them as intruders but welcome them as friends. When trials come, James advises, consider them pure joy, not because they've come but because of what they can develop.

Trials can develop that beautiful trait called perseverance. We might even call it "Christian staying power," the ability to meet the bitterest of life's blows with confident victory. Such staying power is not ours by birth. It needs to be developed in the crucible of life's crises and fired in the furnace of everyday living. Like the maturing oak tree, it needs storm and stress or else it will remain spindly.

Such staying power also gets its start in only one place—in God's Word with its sustaining message of what his love has done for us in Christ. Those who know what God has given them in the Savior will also have the knowledge that he will give them whatever they need in whatever trial he sends.

The Christians of James' day had no corner on the trouble market. Our troubles are as many as the names we carry and as varied as the lives we lead. When those troubles come, our reaction is all important. We dare not let those trials become wedges between us and our gracious God.

They need to be kept on the outside and viewed from long range lest they depress our minds and damage our faith. What trials do for us is the important point, not what they do to us. It is in troubled waters that Christians develop their sea legs. There in the troubled waters we learn that Jesus is both present and precious. When we follow James' practical advice and learn to view trials as tools used by God to develop our Christian perseverance, we can find joy even in them.

A Christian farmer had on his barn a weather vane with the inscription "God is love." An ungodly neighbor scoffed, "So, God's love is as changeable as the wind." "No," the believer replied, "God is love no matter which way the wind blows." One look at our Savior on the cross and we know that God is love. Only when we join James in viewing our trials in the light of that love will we be able to consider them pure joy.

Prayer: Oh, for a faith that will not shrink though
 pressed by many a foe,
That will not tremble on the brink of
 poverty or woe.
Lord, give us such a faith as this, and then,
 whatever may come,
We'll taste even now the hallowed bliss of an
 eternal home. Amen. (CW 405:1,6)

Then Judas (not Judas Iscariot) said, "But, Lord, why do you intend to show yourself to us and not to the world?"

Jesus replied, "If anyone loves me, he will obey my teaching. My Father will love him, and we will come to him and make our home with him."
(John 14:22,23)

Judas, Son of James, the Disciple Who Asked a Question and Received an Answer

"Don't ask so many questions," Grandpa finally told his five-year-old grandson. "What makes peanut butter?" Grandpa could handle. What should he do, though, with, "How do those pictures get on TV?" "What makes grass green?" didn't faze him too much. But how should he answer, "Where do babies come from?"

When it comes to religion, there are also many questions. From our study of Jude perhaps we can learn something about what questions to ask and what to do with the answers we receive.

He asked a question

Two of Jesus' disciples carried the name Judas. Today we don't use this name because of what the one Judas did. Because of him our verses carefully name the one we're studying as "Judas (not Judas Iscariot)." Perhaps the shame attached to the name by the infamous one prompted Matthew and Mark in their accounts to name the other Thaddaeus instead of Judas.

Beyond his name "Judas (not Iscariot)," we have only the question he asked of Jesus that first Maundy Thursday evening. What a dark night that was in mankind's history and also in the hearts of the disciples assembled in the upper room. Their master, whom they loved and whose life they had shared for three years, was talking about dying. His words on the subject were more solemn and determined than any they had heard from him before. And they were afraid. What did all this mean? Where would all this lead? There was so much uncertainty, so many questions.

Judas asked his question, "But, Lord, why do you intend to show yourself to us and not to the world?" Was he thinking back to Palm Sunday when Jesus had ridden into Jerusalem in triumph? Was he asking about an earthly kingdom for Jesus and preferred positions for the disciples in such a kingdom? Was he suggesting: "Lord, now's the time to go out to the people and demonstrate your power. Dazzle them, and, if need be, blast them with your strength so that you can claim the throne of our nation and finally even of the world"?

We've never asked such questions of Jesus? How about those questions of misunderstanding and mistrust that begin with the words, "Lord, why did you . . . ?" or "Lord, why don't you . . . ?" Why did you let that happen to me? Why did you put me in the hospital? Why did you let trouble hit my home? Why did you let my job fizzle out? Why don't you give me success and wealth like that unbelieving neighbor of mine? Why don't you bless me with a mate for life? Why don't you prevent birth defects and rape and crime and wars? With such questions we reveal our inner longing for a Jesus who will offer nickels and dimes for this world instead of his treasures for heaven. With such questions we reveal our proclivity to look to Jesus for a fragrant smelling life instead of a fully cleansed soul.

He received an answer

Judas may have asked the wrong question, but he asked the right person and consequently received the right answer. "If anyone loves me, he will obey my teaching," Jesus replied. "My Father will love him, and we will come to him and make our home with him." Later, after Good Friday with its filled cross and Easter Sunday with its emptied tomb, Judas would understand both the simplicity and the depth of Jesus' answer. Those who would love Jesus must know and hold to his teaching. In his Word Jesus reveals himself as the loving Savior of all. Through that Word people get to know Jesus as their Savior. And those who know and love Jesus and his Word will have him and his Father at their sides. What a comfort for Judas. Wherever his discipleship would take him, whatever he would be called upon to endure, his loving Lord would be with him.

Do we hear what Jesus' answer tells us? Jesus lives and knows how things are with us, not only day by day but hour by hour. Do we have troubles? Is the water in life's boat rising faster than we can bail it out? Jesus knows, and when it's time, from the back of the boat will come his command to the storm, "Peace, be still." Do we face temptations to which we've said, "No," about which we know better, and yet we fall? He knows, and the more we turn to him, the more he will help us tell the old evil foe, "Away from me, Satan." Do we have sins, things we've done that we wish we could forget, but our consciences won't let us? He knows and helps and says, "My blood purifies from every sin." Do we fear death? Do we mouth those words, "We all have to die; keep a stiff upper lip," but inside we're quaking and would rather dodge the grim reaper's scythe? He knows, oh, how he knows, and he who's seen the inside of the tomb himself says, "Because I live, you also will live." These and more are the questions we have, but it's all there in his answer to Judas (not Iscariot). "Love me and my Word," he says, "and my Father and I will be at your side." "Stick close to me," he says, "and we'll stick close to you."

Questions we have and always will, this side of heaven. The point is to know where to turn and whom to ask. When we ask our questions of Jesus, let's also ask for ears wide open to his answers as he speaks them through his Word.

Prayer: Oh, what blessing to be near you and to listen
to your voice!
Let me ever love and fear you; let your Word
still be my choice.
Many hardened sinners, Lord, flee in terror
at your Word,
But to all who feel sin's burden you give peace
and words of pardon. Amen. (CW 283:2)

Reformation Day

"As the rain and the snow
    come down from heaven,
and do not return to it
    without watering the earth
and making it bud and flourish,
    so that it yields seed for the sower and bread for the eater,
so is my word that goes out from my mouth:
    It will not return to me empty,
but will accomplish what I desire
    and achieve the purpose for which I sent it." (Isaiah 55:10,11)

His Word Works

"But does it really work?" You watch that knife sawing through metal on the TV commercial and the next second slicing a tomato. And you can't help asking, "But does it really work?"

Through the ages people have asked the same question about God's Word. Before Martin Luther, the church thought it had to supplement the Word, adding teachings and traditions till the truth was all but buried under such human debris. Then God sent his Reformer to restore the Word to its proper place, with nothing more and nothing less to be taught than it. And the Word worked powerfully in human hearts, as you and I are living, modern proof.

Through the last century, people have again asked with increasing intensity whether the Word works. They've answered by turning away from the Word or attempting to explain it away, as they've modernized it to fit the itching ears of 20th-century people. On a festival like Reformation, it's time for us to hear again what God himself has to say about his Word.

It goes out from God's mouth

"My word," God calls it, and just to make sure we don't miss it, he adds, "that goes out from my mouth." How much more insistent could he be? Men like Isaiah wrote the books of the Bible, but only under the inspiration of God's Spirit. As a result, that's God himself talking to us through those human authors and telling us what he wants us to know.

Do you begin to understand why we can be so confident that his Word works? A man is only as good as his word, states an old adage. How much more so with God. Humans may and often do lie, but God only and always speaks truth. Is it some promise he makes? Sooner will heaven pass away than his promise not be fulfilled. Is it some threat he lays down? Sooner will hell's fires stop burning than his threat not come true. His Word coming out of his mouth is also filled with his power. Get the picture? There will be results when we work with his Word.

How depressing to see around us those who are well on their way to forgetting what the power of the church is. The church's power is not to be found in its social activities or crowd-pleasing events, nor in updating its message and trying to match what people seem to want to hear. The power is in that which goes out from God's mouth—his true and powerful Word! The festival of the Reformation offers the opportunity not only to thank a gracious God for restoring his Word but also to rededicate ourselves to working with it and trusting it to work.

It goes out on God's mission

Only the Lord can send the rain. When he does, he has
a particular purpose in mind. He doesn't send the drops
merely to evaporate and be sucked back up into the sky. They
are sent to water the earth so that seeds can germinate and
plants appear. Later the rain helps the stalks to ripen and the
harvest to come. The result is new seed for the sower and
bread for the eater. That's the mission on which God sends
the rain and snow. But he sends them where and how he
wants; he causes them to work where and when he pleases.

Again, get the picture? The Word that goes out from God's
mouth goes out on his mission, one we could summarize
with three *R*s. The first purpose of the Word is *revelation*.
Just as we use words to reveal ourselves to others, so does
God. Without his Word we would not know him as the
triune God, majestic in his being and marvelously intent on
our salvation. The second is *redemption*. On the pages of his
Word beats the loving, caring, saving heart of God who so
loved a damnation-deserving world that he sent his Son to
die for it. The third is *regeneration*. The Word is the Holy
Spirit's tool for blasting open stony hearts of unbelief and
planting faith. It is also the Spirit's tool for causing the shoot
of faith to grow and mature, producing fruit that shows in a
daily life both cross dimensioned and heaven directed.

Note carefully: It's God's mission. He uses the Word to
accomplish what he desires and achieve the purpose for
which he sends it. We cannot tell God where or how or
in what way or in whom his Word should work. But we
can work with his Word, and we can trust that his Word
will work because he himself has promised it will not
return empty.

After years of hard work and meager results, Missionary Guenther on April 30, 1922, was ready to dedicate the first chapel at Whiteriver, Arizona, on the Apache reservation. Imagine his surprise and happiness when Apache Chief Alchesay came forward for Baptism in that service and was followed by one hundred members of his tribe. The chief told the assembly, "This is the only church I've put my mark on. You listen to that tall missionary when he speaks from the Book." That same chief on his deathbed asked for the shawl in which was wrapped the key to the Whiteriver church. Taking the key, he said, "This is the key that opened the door to God's house. This is the key that opened the door to heaven." The Word works!

Every pastor and missionary can relate similar stories about the Word working in the hearts of people, sometimes the least expected ones, sometimes at the most unexpected times. So can all of us when we look back at how the Word has worked in our own hearts.

Time to say it again: "Thank you, Lord, for the great reformer, Martin Luther. Even more so, thank you, Lord, for the Word, the only power that works." Time also to ask it again: "Please, Lord, keep that Word in our midst and help us trust its power."

Prayer: Thank you, Lord, for restoring and keeping your precious Word in our midst. Thank you for making us wise unto salvation through it. Help us treasure, use, and spread that powerful message of your love and trust it to work in human hearts. Amen.

All Saints' Day (November 1)

After this I looked and there before me was a great multitude that no one could count, from every nation, tribe, people, and language, standing before the throne and in front of the Lamb. They were wearing white robes and were holding palm branches in their hands. And they cried out in a loud voice:

> "Salvation belongs to our God,
> who sits on the throne,
> and to the Lamb."

All the angels were standing around the throne and around the elders and the four living creatures. They fell down on their faces before the throne and worshiped God, saying:

> "Amen!
> Praise and glory
> and wisdom and thanks and honor
> and power and strength
> be to our God for ever and ever.
> Amen!"

Then one of the elders asked me, "These in white robes—who are they, and where did they come from?"

I answered, "Sir, you know."

And he said, "These are they who have come out of the great tribulation; they have washed their robes and made them white in the blood of the Lamb. Therefore,

> "they are before the throne of God
> and serve him day and night in his temple;
> and he who sits on the throne will spread his tent over them.
> Never again will they hunger;
> never again will they thirst.
> The sun will not beat upon them,
> nor any scorching heat.

For the Lamb at the center of the throne will be their shepherd;
he will lead them to springs of living water.
And God will wipe away every tear from their eyes."
(Revelation 7:9-17)

Something to Sing About

"Who wants to go to heaven if all they do there is sing?"
asked the teenager. Heaven appealed to her, and, yes, she
did want to spend eternity with her Savior. But the thought
of singing throughout eternity didn't quite make it with her.

It's true, the Scriptures do speak about believers singing in
heaven. When we look closely, though, we note that it is
not so much the singing that is stressed but to whom and
about what we will sing.

To whom?

"Salvation belongs to our God . . . and to the Lamb," we'll
sing in heaven. To God we'll give the glory in heaven. To
our gracious, saving God, we'll sing throughout eternity,
with the holy angels joining in.

Why to God? Because he will have brought us to heaven,
the place where there is no more sin. That's what our
wearing "white robes" is all about. John, just as we do at
times, uses the color white to express purity. In heaven
there will be no more evil heart within us trying to lure us
into sin, no more devil and his evil angels trying to trip us
up, no more temptations, period! Instead, we will be pure,
sinless, holy like the angels of God.

Why to God? Because he will have brought us to heaven, the place where there will be no more heat of trouble or tears of sorrow. Gone will be the trials and the troubles that on this earth beat down upon us like the scorching rays of the desert sun, threatening to parch our faith and melt our souls. Instead, our gentle Shepherd will give us all we need to be eternally happy, and even the thought of that last earthly tear will be erased from our eyes.

Why to God? Because he will have brought us to heaven, the place where he is constantly with us and where we can serve him perfectly. Gone will be the days when, even though we knew Jesus was with us, we wished we could see him face-to-face. In heaven we will see his face, with all his rich love shining forth. Here on earth we catch a glimpse of that love in his Holy Word, like some snapshot, but in heaven the height of our joy will be to see our Savior face-to-face.

To whom will we sing the heavenly hymn? Joyous voices, triumphant faith, complete knowledge will raise the mighty hymn to a gracious, glorious God for giving us unworthy sinners a place at his side in a wonderful heaven. Here on earth we sing already, but so often off-key because of our sinful hearts. In heaven with all the angels who have ever been there and with all the saints who have gone before, we'll join a perfect hymn of praise.

By whom?

Who will sing that hymn? "A great multitude," John said, "from every nation, tribe, people, and language." Note carefully that John did not say that all people from every nation, tribe, people, and language would be in heaven. He limited it to those who "have washed their robes and made them white in the blood of the Lamb." Those who do laundry can well understand John's picture. It takes the right detergent to remove the dirt of daily wear from our clothing. So John also speaks of dirt and detergents. Only his reference is to the dirt of sin, the grease and grime of daily life that is ground into and soils our souls. He was writing about the mud and muck of sinful birth and sinful life that dresses every human being only for hell.

The right detergent? John is very clear about that also. It's the "blood of the Lamb." No other detergent will do. The soap of man's own works can only set sin's stain instead of removing it. Only Christ's precious blood can cleanse from sin. And only those who have had their sin-stained souls washed in his blood, that is, only believers, will be in heaven singing the glorious hymn of praise to the Lamb. Not everyone who believes in something will be in that heavenly choir, but only those who by God's grace believe in Jesus as their one and only Savior from sin.

Something to sing about? Absolutely! Let's not wait till heaven to begin. Let's start right here and now.

Prayer: O Lord, take our voices and let us sing, ever, only for our King, here and in heaven. Amen.

St. Andrew, Apostle (November 30)

The next day John was there again with two of his disciples. When he saw Jesus passing by, he said, "Look, the Lamb of God!"

When the two disciples heard him say this, they followed Jesus.

Turning around, Jesus saw them following and asked, "What do you want?"

They said, "Rabbi" (which means Teacher), "where are you staying?"

"Come," he replied, "and you will see."

So they went and saw where he was staying, and spent that day with him. It was about the tenth hour.

Andrew, Simon Peter's brother, was one of the two who heard what John had said and who had followed Jesus. The first thing Andrew did was to find his brother Simon and tell him, "We have found the Messiah" (that is, the Christ). And he brought him to Jesus. (John 1:35-42)

Andrew, the Disciple We Want to Follow in the Father's Business

How often do we reach our goals? New parents gazing through the nursery window have ideas about that precious package brought to them by God. "An engineer or computer expert, a teacher or a star," they dream of for their child.

Teenagers have their dreams too. "A pro basketball star scoring in double digits or a semi driver pulling a big rig across the US, a celebrated musician or famous novelist" might be in their plans.

Goals and dreams may vary widely. Final results may turn out far differently. Yet in one area every believer surely would want to be the same. Every believer would want to follow Andrew in the heavenly Father's business.

With a faith that grows

"Andrew," we might ask, "tell us something about yourself." In answer, he might talk about something we often take for granted, about the day he met Jesus. "I'll never forget that day," he might say. "Oh, yes, we knew something about Jesus. Our teacher John the Baptist had seen to that. But that day when John actually pointed his finger at him, what a day that turned out to be. We just simply had to follow Jesus. What a feeling it was when he spoke to us and invited us in. I can still remember the time. For you 21st-century people with digital watches it was about 4:00 P.M. when we sat down with him. Even more, I'll never forget what he talked about that day."

Are we imagining too much if we were to hear Andrew go on: "Do you know what Jesus talked about? The same thing he talked about with the woman at the well in Samaria and with Nicodemus in the upper room. He told us he was the Lamb of God, the one for whom we had been waiting, the one who would bear our sins and pay for them. You should have heard him open the Scriptures. Why, your heart would have burned within you too that day."

Want to be like Andrew? No, the question is not whether we can pinpoint the day and hour when we first met Jesus. Watch out for those who want to stress the time of conversion and who go on and on about being born again. So often such a stress indicates unhealthy shifting from the Christ in whom we believe to the *me* who believes. Andrew would be the first to put the emphasis where it belongs, on Christ and his Word and on God's grace in bringing people to the Savior.

"You don't want to stop just with knowing Jesus," Andrew might continue. "The more you hear him speak through his Word, the more you will get to know him and love him and benefit from him. And then you'll be doing just what my brother told you to do in his second epistle. You'll grow in the grace and knowledge of our Lord and Savior Jesus Christ" (2 Peter 3:18).

With a faith that shows

"I thought of my brother right away," Andrew might go on. "I just had to tell him. I just couldn't think of him not sharing the joy I had in Jesus. And you know what Peter became," Andrew might say with a note of joy in his voice. "He became our spokesman and preached the sermon on Pentecost through which the Holy Spirit brought many to Jesus." If we were to jog his memory, Andrew might recall others to whom he spoke about Jesus, like those Greeks in John chapter 12. But his concern was not to run up a tally or show off his success. It was to bring people to Jesus.

What might your pastor ask for if given a wish? It might be, "Lord, give me a church full of Andrews. Give me parents whose foremost concern is not dental appointments and designer jeans or the right clothes and right careers, but leading their children to Jesus.

"Give me families who tackle the task of telling a spouse or relative about the Savior and his church, about heaven and hell and who model their faith as one way of telling.

"Also, Lord, give me members who realize with a shudder of concern that the unreached millions in our world are going to hell, that mission work is not a hobby at which to play but a driving concern in the lifeblood of our faith.

"Can I have Andrews on our church boards," he might continue, "men who calmly and unassumingly will serve you with everything they have?

"And, Lord, just one more thing. Please give me more Andrews among our young people. Lord, I know they're out there. I can point to some of them, but I ask that you also point to them, that you touch their hearts and kindle in them a desire to serve you as pastors and teachers. Touch also the hearts of their parents and grandparents so that they offer encouragement and help. Show us all the joy that Andrew found in leading others to you."

Goals may change and dreams fail to materialize. Not this one! Lord, help us all to follow Andrew in your business.

Prayer: Lord Jesus, thank you for making Andrews out of us by bringing us to faith. Draw us more into your Word that our faith may grow and then also show in telling others about you. Fill us with the joy of salvation so that we are on fire with the desire to point others to you, the Lamb of God who takes away the sins of the world. Amen.

A week later his disciples were in the house again, and Thomas was with them. Though the doors were locked, Jesus came and stood among them and said, "Peace be with you!" Then he said to Thomas, "Put your finger here; see my hands. Reach out your hand and put it into my side. Stop doubting and believe."

Thomas said to him, "My Lord and my God!"

Then Jesus told him, "Because you have seen me, you have believed; blessed are those who have not seen and yet have believed." (John 20:26-29)

Thomas, the Disciple to Whom We Are Twin

We're much like Thomas, do you know that? No, not that we carry his name, though some of us might. In Greek he was called Didymus, in Hebrew, Thomas, both meaning "twin." To whom he was a twin we aren't told. In fact, Matthew, Mark, and Luke in their gospels give us no more than his name. It's in John's gospel that we learn more about him and especially in the verses before us. Looking more closely at that account will reveal why we could often be called Thomas' twin.

In asking our questions

Poor Thomas had missed it. He had not been present that first Easter evening to see the risen Lord as the other disciples had. All week long the others had tried to tell him, but he just wouldn't believe them. "Unless I see the nail marks in his hands and put my finger where the nails were, and put my hand into his side, I will not believe it," he objected. Thomas was making a statement, a rather firm statement, but in reality he was asking a question. His haunting question was, "You don't really expect me to believe that Jesus is no longer dead, do you?"

We could be Thomas' twin. Even on Easter, perhaps especially on Easter, we ask our questions about death. Some of us are more candid and ask them out loud. Others of us mull them over silently where only our hearts can hear. But we ask them! We connect with death the greatest question marks in life.

Sometimes the question takes the form of blunt denial. "Don't talk like that," we bluster when a loved one tries to speak about death. Other times we try to cover up the question with semantics, calling death "passing away" or "going to rest." A few even claim to face the question head-on with bluffing words like "when you're dead, you're dead." But we wonder what they're really feeling inside.

If we are honest, we'll have to admit that those questions about death often bother us. The point isn't that we should never have such questions. Our Jesus never said to Thomas and he never says to us, "Ask *no* questions, have *no* doubts." He knows our weak and feeble mortal natures too well for that. The point is that he wants us to know where to go with those questions and whom to ask. The point is that we do what Thomas did, ask the risen Savior and then also like Thomas believe the answers Jesus gives us in his Word.

In believing Jesus' answers

Thomas had asked for nail prints and a spear wound. One week later he received the evidence in overwhelming, convincing reality. For on that Sunday after Easter, the risen

Savior came again, this time looking especially for Thomas. "Thomas," he said, "put your finger here; see my hands. Reach out your hand and put it into my side. Stop doubting and believe." Almost before the gentle voice had finished speaking, Thomas was on his knees at the nail-pierced feet, saying, "My Lord and my God!" It was all he could say and it was enough. He was seeing the living Lord. Now he understood those earlier words about the Father's house and the one way to it. Now he knew sin's payment was finished and heaven's road built, laid and paved with the Savior's atoning blood. No wonder he exclaimed in humble faith, "My Lord and my God."

Neither the gospels nor the book of Acts tell us specifically what happened to Thomas after that fateful evening. Tradition relates that he spent the rest of his days in far-off India, preaching the message of the risen Jesus and then dying as a martyr. Scripture does, however, detail how others who saw the living Lord and trusted his answers walked in loving service to him. The humble confession, "My Lord and my God," is lived out in willing service wherever God places the believer in life.

So what if in the days ahead the threat of war doesn't disappear, the economy slows down, tornadoes and floods and earthquakes occur in the world and in our circle of life. So what? "My Lord and my God," we join Thomas in saying in humble trust. He lives to silence all our fears.

So what if death's cold knuckles come knocking at our doors. So what if a loved one is left under that fresh mound at the cemetery. So what if we count down our days one by one in the current year or whatever year is put before us. So what?

"My Lord and my God," we join Thomas in saying in humble trust. He lives and we shall conquer death.

So what if life continues at the same pace and in the same comfortable groove. So what if our circumstances do not alter nor our steps falter. Let the answer then not be a complacent "So what?" but instead a challenge to live for the living Lord. Let the response of humble faith be: "Savior, I long to walk closer with thee. . . . Living for him who died freely for me" (CW 473:4).

Twins of Thomas, that's us. Not only in asking our questions but even more so in believing the risen Savior's answers.

Prayer: Thank you, risen Savior, for showing us the glorious truths of your resurrection in the pages of your Holy Word. Help us believe what we have seen and trust you for forgiveness, peace, and heaven. Help us also live as ones who have the answers we need for life and death in our living Savior. In your name we ask it. Amen.

St. Stephen, Deacon and Martyr (December 26)

Now Stephen, a man full of God's grace and power, did great wonders and miraculous signs among the people. Opposition arose, however, from members of the Synagogue of the Freedmen (as it was called)—Jews of Cyrene and Alexandria as well as the provinces of Cilicia and Asia. These men began to argue with Stephen, but they could not stand up against his wisdom or the Spirit by whom he spoke.

So they stirred up the people and the elders and the teachers of the law. They seized Stephen and brought him before the Sanhedrin.

All who were sitting in the Sanhedrin looked intently at Stephen, and they saw that his face was like the face of an angel. (Acts 6:8-10,12,15)

A Power Shortage? Look at Stephen!

The power was out. The electric lines, whipped by the wind, had gone down, and the power was out. At first, it was almost peaceful as the house quieted down with all the appliances stopped. But then came the problems. How would we keep the ice cream frozen or prepare dinner or watch TV?

The Bible reference for the day after Christmas, known as St. Stephen's Day, also talks about a power shortage, or even more specifically, about what to do to avoid one. From Stephen comes an example of where to find the spiritual power we need and what to do with that power.

Power to speak up for Christ

Stephen was on trial for his life before the Sanhedrin, the same court that Jesus had faced. How did he get there? Because he wouldn't be quiet. His enemies even said this. Remember Stephen's background? When the apostles needed help in managing the affairs in the large congregation at

Jerusalem, they chose deacons to work with them. Stephen was one of those selected, and he served willingly, doing whatever he could. We soon find him witnessing in the various synagogues in Jerusalem. People flocked to hear him because he spoke with a Bible wisdom given him by the Spirit. Though prominent members of the synagogues challenged him, they couldn't silence him. Finally, there was only one way to turn off Stephen's effective witnessing about the Savior. That was to kill this man who they claimed never stopped speaking.

Do you think it was easy for Stephen to stand up and speak up for Christ in the midst of those who also had been enemies of the Savior? Where did he get the power? Aren't we told in those words that described him as "a man full of God's grace and power" and the words that referred to the "wisdom or the Spirit by whom he spoke"? Stephen was wired. He had the right connection to Christ. The only way to know Christ is through the Word. The only true wisdom is found in the Word. The closer the Spirit connects one with Christ and his Word, the more the believer has the power needed to speak up about Christ.

What about our power connection? We may not have talents such as the Spirit gave Stephen, but we do have opportunities to speak up for Christ. Do we even need to talk about such speaking up? As one missionary put it, "Why all this theological talk about missions and witnessing? It's simple. You witness because you must. A new baby is born—it cries. A man is born in Christ—he witnesses. The more a baby cries, the more you know it is a good, healthy baby. The Christian is just like that."

If this past year we at times were silent when we should have spoken up, afraid when we should have been bold, perhaps it's time to check our power connection. From Stephen we learn that Christ and his Word furnish the power we need to speak up about the Savior.

Power to suffer for Christ

On trial for his life, Stephen might have been expected to plead his innocence with fear and trembling. Instead, he boldly witnessed of the Savior whom God had promised and then sent and whom they had murdered. Such was the power of the faith within him that his face reflected some of the light of heaven and the glory of Christ. When his judges looked at him, they saw "the face of an angel."

Stephen's words struck home, but instead of drinking in the life-giving gospel, his enemies rushed like hungry wolves on their helpless victim, dragged him out of the city, and stoned him till he lay a mangled corpse at their feet. That was only the beginning. In their fury they began a great persecution against all Christians in Jerusalem, ruthlessly scattering them throughout Judea and Samaria in a fanatic but futile attempt to wipe out any trace of the Savior's name.

What about our power connection? We may not be called upon to give up our lives as Stephen did. Yet if we really speak out for Christ, we'll feel the sting of persecution. Ask the college student who heads out of the dorm for church on Sunday morning if he'll receive any flak. Ask the teenager who refuses to smoke pot, swill alcohol, or sleep around whether there'll be any repercussions. Ask the business person who operates honestly following Christian principles whether he'll be appreciated. Ask the pastor pointing the finger of God's law at a member sinking in sin whether he'll be invited in cheerfully and gracefully given a cup of coffee. Speaking up for Christ and his Word has never been easy. Stephen would tell us that. We'll know it too as we try it in a world that no longer frowns on sin, but legitimizes it and that no longer respects, but ridicules the master's followers.

Are we ready to speak up for Christ even if it means suffering? "The power," we ask, "where does it come from?" Look at Stephen. His source is our source. His power and ours come from Christ and his Word. The better our connection to Christ and his Word, the greater our power will be even to suffer for Christ.

Prayer: Lord Jesus, thank you for bleeding and dying for us. Like Stephen of old, we ask that you strengthen our faith. Give it the concern it needs to witness of you, the only Redeemer, and the courage necessary to do this in the face of opposition and ridicule. Through your Word give us power to live for you and to die in you so that with Stephen we may see the glories of heaven. Amen.

We love because he first loved us. (1 John 4:19)

John, the Disciple Who Teaches Us about a Love That's Real

Most people couldn't tell that the $20 bills were phony. That's why it took a while before the counterfeiters were caught. Something similar happens with the item described as "love." Aided by media that describe love in terms of indiscriminate sex and pleasure upon demand, our world has opted for the counterfeit. For so many, love means getting instead of giving.

How different is the love God displays and asks us to imitate, as John, the apostle of love, reminds us.

Christ's love for us

Carefully and lovingly the master shaped him, molding his faith. In the bedroom of Jairus' house, John saw death conquered. On the Mount of Transfiguration, he previewed heaven's glory. In the Garden of Gethsemane, he witnessed the sin-bearer's agony. The results of such shaping showed on Maundy Thursday evening as John was the first of the panic-stricken disciples to rally. Though Peter followed afar off, John courageously entered the courtyard of the high priest's palace. Though all the disciples the next day huddled behind locked doors, John alone out of the Twelve hovered with several women beneath the Savior's cross.

Why? How come? What brought this all about? John himself gives the answer as he points always to the Savior and never to himself. Not once in the gospel that he authored does he list himself by name, though the three other evangelists mention him some 30 times. Five times he refers to himself as the "disciple whom Jesus loved," three times as "that other" or "another disciple," but never as John. Always, though, he points to Jesus. Someone said that in the fourth gospel, John is never visible and Jesus is never invisible. And when John points to Jesus, so often he points to his great love.

It's as if John were saying, "Do you want to know how come I became Jesus' disciple? How come I would never leave him? How come he's my greatest treasure? How come I stood beneath his cross and will stand before his throne in heaven? Then don't look at me. It had nothing to do with me. It was all Jesus and his love. In love he chose me. In love he laid down his life for me. In love he keeps me close to him. Yes, in love *he gives himself to me.*"

Thank God, his love for us is a no-strings-attached love, not one conditioned on what we are or what he could get from us. If it were, just think how he would have to tell us, "I hate you and want nothing to do with you." Instead, John, the apostle of love, reminds us, "This is love: not that we loved God, but that he loved us and sent his Son as an atoning sacrifice for our sins" (1 John 4:10). Now that's a love that's real, a love that's absolutely concerned about giving, not getting.

One night a popular medieval priest announced he would preach a sermon on God's love. Quietly the people sat for some time in the darkening cathedral, wondering, "When will the service start and we hear that sermon about God's love?" Finally, when the great church was entirely dark, the priest lit one candle and walked over to the life-sized crucifix behind the altar. He held the candle to each of the pierced hands, to the spiked feet, to the stabbed side, and then to the thorn-crowned head, as the congregation rose silently, reverently to its feet. That was his sermon on the love of God, a love that's real. To him who gave his all upon that cross, John points us. "He first loved us," John reminds us.

Our love for Christ

Those who have felt the sunshine of divine love reflect it. "We love [him]," John wrote simply, "because he first loved us." Love moved John to stand beneath his Savior's cross even though the others fled. When the Sanhedrin ordered John "not to speak or teach at all in the name of Jesus," love moved him to answer, "We cannot help speaking about what we have seen and heard" (Acts 4:18-20). Even when the consequences meant being exiled to the rugged island of Patmos, John's love would not let him be silent about his Savior. Service to the Savior was the purpose of his life. The Holy Spirit even used this service to bring us five books of the New Testament, in which John testified clearly and sweetly about the Savior who first loved us.

John, like an eagle, not only soared to greater heights than any other in speaking of God's love; he also stayed very practically on earth. From him comes the reminder that the best way to show love to God is to show it to those whom God has placed around us. "Anyone who does not love his brother, whom he has seen, cannot love God, whom he has not seen," he tells us (1 John 4:20). "Dear friends," he urges us again and again, "love one another" (1 John 4:7).

Loving God means putting his commandments first in our lives and trying gladly to bring our lives into line with them. Loving God means giving him the first place he wants in our hearts and showing it with our priorities. Loving God means reaching that point in faith where he is not just someone from whom we get so much but someone to whom we want to give our all. Loving God means loving those whom he has placed around us, showing concern not for what we can get from them but for what we can give to them, not for what they can do for us but for what we can do for them.

Hard? Of course. It's almost impossible at times in a world where counterfeit love reigns supreme—until we take the little candle of faith and hold it up before the pierced hands and spiked feet, the stabbed side and crowned head of the One who first loved us.

Prayer: Lord, teach us more about the height and depth and length and breadth of your love that moved you to give your life for us. Then help us reflect that unselfish love in our dealings with one another and in our words and works for you. Amen.

The Holy Innocents, Martyrs (December 28)

When Herod realized that he had been outwitted by the Magi, he was furious, and he gave orders to kill all the boys in Bethlehem and its vicinity who were two years old and under, in accordance with the time he had learned from the Magi. Then what was said through the prophet Jeremiah was fulfilled:

"A voice is heard in Ramah,
  weeping and great mourning,
Rachel weeping for her children
  and refusing to be comforted,
because they are no more."

After Herod died, an angel of the Lord appeared in a dream to Joseph in Egypt and said, "Get up, take the child and his mother and go to the land of Israel, for those who were trying to take the child's life are dead." (Matthew 2:16-20)

They'll Only Lose

What a depressing account, coming after the beautiful news of the Savior's birth at Bethlehem. A cruel tyrant schemes; the holy family is forced to flee to a foreign country; innocent little children are senselessly and brutally murdered. What's to be learned from such a dark episode? What kind of gain for us from such gruesome details? Not much, we say? Then let's look again and find the comforting truth that when foolish men take on God, they always lose.

Foolish men keep trying

Can we even imagine the feverish alarm in hell when the Savior was born? The devil knew why the Christ Child had come and wasn't going to give up without a battle. In hellish rage Satan geared up for the battle against the Lord's Anointed and found a ready ally in King Herod.

Outwitted by the Magi, Herod reacts with predictable rage. Cleverly he calculates from the time the Magi had seen the star in the East. Shrewdly he gives himself enough leeway, adding a bit more just to be sure. Out from the brutal butcher goes the command that all the baby boys of Bethlehem from the age of two years downward be slaughtered. How many babies did he kill? Bethlehem wasn't that big, so neither was the number. But even one of those innocent babies, guilty of no crime against the king, would have been too many. Even one was enough to bring the sound of wailing to the streets of that little town of Bethlehem.

The prophet Jeremiah had foretold this weeping (Jeremiah 31:15). He saw Rachel, Jacob's favored wife who had remained childless for so long, watching from her grave and wailing when her descendants, the Israelites, were gathered in the camps at Ramah to be carried away into captivity in the East (40:1). Now Matthew applies this prophecy also to the bloody scene at Bethlehem, picturing Rachel as joining the mourning over the senseless murder of those innocent children.

Blood flowed and tears fell that mournful night in Bethlehem. To the outward eye, an evil, brutal man had his little day, seemingly triumphant. In our day too. When little ones, before even seeing the light of day, are ripped out of the womb by tearing forceps or burning solution; when citizens of the same country slaughter one another in the name of ethnic cleansing; when enemies stalk the earth seeking to cancel God's will; when justice and truth are trampled underfoot; when God's people seem to have reason only for weeping; we have to admit we wonder at times. Has God lost his grip? Does he no longer care? Has he abdicated his throne and left us to stew in our own juices? When such questions come, then it's time to read on and get the rest of the story.

A faithful God keeps triumphing

A faithful God was still very much in control. When it was his time, an angel was sent to inform the holy family in Egypt, "Get up, take the child and his mother and go to the land of Israel, for those who were trying to take the child's life are dead." Of course, the Lord could have prevented the flight into Egypt by ending Herod's life earlier. Instead, he chose this way to show that he was in control. He also chose this way to bring Jeremiah's prophecy to fulfillment. Dare we say that he even did it this way to teach us something about his promises and his protection of us? When the battle is over and the smoke clears, we'll find a faithful God still standing and very much in control.

Is there any comfort in this truth for us when we look at our world, which is seemingly out of control? The devil used Herod in his day to try and wipe out the Christ Child. In our day it's no secret that such efforts have not slowed down, but rather speeded up. In our country the devil uses the 'isms—materialism with its mad chase after earthly treasures, hedonism with its relentless pursuit of pleasure, individualism with its shortsighted view that what seems true to me is true—to try to strangle the gospel. Elsewhere Satan uses ridicule, criticism, edicts, even the sword against the Lord's Anointed. But the gospel still goes out to the ends of the earth, and weary souls still find the rest they need. Those who seek to destroy Jesus have their little day, but he lives on forever.

Any comfort in this truth when we look at our own lives? Sometimes we feel that the Lord has lost his faithfulness. That he no longer looks down on us or, if he does, that he overlooks us. That he's too busy managing the universe to be concerned about little entities like us. Anxiously we ask, "Does he care?" Ceaselessly the world scoffs, "Where is your God?" We hurry our prayers to his throne only seemingly to find the heavens sealed. But not even a sparrow falls without his knowledge. His clock keeps different time than ours, and his ways are so much superior to ours. As the years roll round, we learn more and more to be still and know that he is God, our faithful God, who "moves in a mysterious way his wonders to perform."

And when we still can't quite see his hand, then it's time to look again at the cross of his Son. There we see how much he really cares and how faithful he really is. He who sent his only Son to Calvary that we might have life with him in heaven will not let anything pluck us out of his hands here on earth. Knowing that precious truth, we know enough.

Prayer: Eternal Lord, in whose loving hands we live and move and have our being, help us raise our eyes above the smoke and turmoil of this world to you. Show us again your love in Christ Jesus so that we trust that love in the lesser areas of our lives. Use us to spread the message of your greatest triumph over sin and Satan through the death and rising again of your Son, so that others may share in the heavenly victory at your side. In Jesus' name we ask it. Amen.

New Year's Eve

I will lift up my eyes to the hills—
where does my help come from?
My help comes from the LORD,
the Maker of heaven and earth. (Psalm 121:1,2)

Changing Years the Right Way

Changing years is easy, isn't it? All we have to do is throw out the old calendar and take out the new. And then don't forget to write the new number the next few days. What's so hard about that?

For the thinking person, it's not quite that simple. Parts of the past year he or she would just as soon forget, but erasing them is not so easy. How do you remove from the mind the tension and trouble, the problems and sins of the year gone by? Nor is stepping off into the dark unknown of a new year a light matter. Such a person welcomes advice about changing years the right way.

Look up, not down

"I will lift up my eyes to the hills—where does my help come from?" the psalmist said. With these words he wasn't urging us to love mountains or seek to climb them. Instead, he was saying, "Look up beyond the hills on which Jerusalem was built with its holy temple. Look much higher, up to the Lord who made those hills."

It's not easy to look up. We'd much rather follow the lead of the world and look down—at ourselves. From little on we do this. "I do it myself," pouts the little one whose shoe you are trying to tie. "Leave me alone," responds the teenager to whom you are trying to give advice. "That's not the way we do it," objects the senior citizen when changes are proposed. Human beings tend to look down at themselves and all too often Christians tend to follow their lead.

Now listen to the psalmist. He did not write, "My help comes from *me*." It's, "My help comes from the LORD." Forget this, and we are in trouble. Who are we that we can help ourselves? How mighty is our right arm and how foolproof our plans? How often this past year didn't we fret and even fail because we looked in the wrong direction? How cautious and concerned aren't we already about the new year because we look down at insufficient mortals instead of up at an almighty God?

Want to change years the right way? Then don't look down. Look up—at God. He made heaven and earth. He surely can and will take care of us. We can trust him.

Look back, then ahead

Changing years involves also a backward look. So often the danger in looking backwards is that we see only the troubles because they etch themselves deeper into our memories. But tell me, were there no joys as the year sped so swiftly by? No moments of meaningful love shared with spouse or children? No proper pride in the achievements and advancements of family members? No successes in our jobs or professions? No lighter moments on the lake or at the ball game? No comfort from a church service where the sermon seemed tailored just for us? What about such joys? Let's not forget from whom such blessings flowed and how easily he can grant them also in the new year, if they should be for our good and his glory.

Does the backward look involve something painful? Were there times when we blew it in our dealings with others, perhaps even with those closest to us? Times when we tried so hard and yet fell right back into sin's old ruts and felt so bad afterwards? Times when people we cared for were hurting or in the hospital? Times when the load of trouble seemed two hundred pounds heavier than we could carry? Times when we just couldn't get a grip on our depressed or down feelings?

"Look back," the psalmist tells us, "look back and see where some of those problems are now." Many of them are gone, lifted by the loving hand of an almighty God. Some may still be with us, yet we made it through the year in spite of them. A gracious God helped us bear them and even grow because of them. From burdens not removed come muscles of faith, like those of the weight lifter, strengthened by the continued carrying. From storms that keep blowing come roots of faith, like those of the pines on the mountainside, sunk deeper into the soil of God's Word. From the sandpaper of troubles that keep rubbing against us comes a polished faith, like the wood grain on a fine piece of furniture. "Look back," the psalmist tells us, "look back at them and realize who still sends them and why he does."

Looking back will also help us look ahead. Some people as they look back see only trouble and as they look ahead see only uncertainty. Not the children of God. If we remember what a faithful God did for us in just half of the days gone by, we will have confidence to trust God to do much the same in the new year. Such confidence is not based on our knowing what might happen to us or who of us will still be here when the next year rolls around. It comes from knowing not what the new year holds, but who holds the new year. It's the Lord who went all out to save us and whom we can trust now to go all out to fill the new year with what he knows is good for us. His love and forgiveness and concern do not change with the calendar.

When we look at him, changing years is easy.

Prayer: Eternal Father, today we look back and see your goodness that surrounded every step we took in the year gone by. Help us enter the new year, trusting in the name of your Son and walking in the way of his peace, with your Word as the lamp to our feet and the light to our path. Then we know our year will be happy and our future secure. Amen.

Calendar of Minor Festivals

January

1 The Name of Jesus
18 The Confession of St. Peter
24 St. Timothy, Pastor and
    Confessor
25 The Conversion of St. Paul
26 St. Titus, Pastor and Confessor

February

2 The Presentation of Our Lord
24 St. Matthias, Apostle

March

19 St. Joseph
25 The Annunciation of Our Lord

April

25 St. Mark, Evangelist

May

1 St. Philip and St. James,
    Apostles
31 The Visitation

June

11 St. Barnabas, Apostle
24 The Nativity of St. John
    the Baptist
25 Presentation of the Augsburg
    Confession
29 St. Peter and St. Paul, Apostles

July

22 St. Mary Magdalene
25 St. James the Elder, Apostle

August

15 St. Mary, Mother of Our Lord
24 St. Bartholomew, Apostle

September

21 St. Matthew, Apostle
29 St. Michael and All Angels

October

18 St. Luke, Evangelist
23 St. James of Jerusalem
28 St. Simon and St. Jude,
    Apostles
31 Reformation Day

November

1 All Saints' Day
30 St. Andrew, Apostle

December

21 St. Thomas, Apostle
26 St. Stephen, Deacon and
    Martyr
27 St. John, Apostle and
    Evangelist
28 The Holy Innocents, Martyrs
31 New Year's Eve